ABINGDON'S BOARDINGHOUSE MURDER

GREG LILLY

THE
History
PRESS

Published by The History Press
Charleston, SC
www.historypress.com

First published 2024

Manufactured in the United States

ISBN 9781467157322

Library of Congress Control Number: 2024931454

To the Clark and Newton families and their descendants.
This tragic situation was the combination of two shell-shocked and lonely people,
the morals of the 1940s, the societal trauma caused by World War II and a
series of events that might have changed with a single decision.

CONTENTS

Preface 7
Acknowledgements 9

1. The Murder... 11
2. Vista Ellen "Helen" Talbert Clark.. 19
3. James "Jimmy" Emmett Newton Jr. 41
4. The Instigator: Genoa Kathleen "Kitty" Smyth 60
5. The Model Family/Son Next Door: Andrew Summers.................. 63
6. The Snowstorm: Abingdon, Virginia, December 1944.................... 67
7. The Good Times: New Smyrna, Florida,
    Winter/Spring 1945 76
8. Settling in as Brother/Son/Lover: Abingdon, Virginia,
    Summer 1945.. 83
9. The Coach and the Widow: Abingdon and Damascus, Virginia,
    Fall 1945 90
10. Jimmy's Last Day: Abingdon, Virginia, Sunday,
    November 18, 1945...93
11. The Investigation and Arrest: Abingdon, Virginia,
    November 19–November 20, 1945 101
12. The Community Whispers: Abingdon, Virginia,
    November 21, 1945–May 5, 1946 108

CONTENTS

13. The Trial: Abingdon, Virginia, May 6–May 13, 1946 113
14. The Murderess and the Aftermath....................................... 128
15. The Rumors and Scenarios 132

Bibliography 141
About the Author 143

PREFACE

A couple of years ago, I attended a Fourth of July cookout at the notorious "Murder House" on Abingdon's Valley Street. All the neighbors had stories to tell of the killing of a twenty-two-year-old World War II marine who boarded with a forty-four-year-old widow and her three daughters. Some tales were shocking, some fantastical and others scandalous.

Newspaper coverage of the 1945 murder, investigation and trial revealed the facts and the fascination the nation had with the crime. The 1950 movie *Sunset Boulevard*, written by Billy Wilder, Charles Brackett and D.M. Marshman, parallels some plot points from this crime. Did the screenwriters borrow themes from these events? The Clark trial had been splashed across newspaper headlines a couple of years before that screenplay was developed.

The local historical society holds family stories and archives of town newspapers and events, along with staff who have heard even more rumors from their parents and grandparents. I wanted a firsthand account. I searched for descendants of the widow Clark. The oldest granddaughter of the widow, to my surprise, had been my high school science teacher Ms. Gay Leonard. I interviewed her about her grandmother, her mother (who was the widow's eldest daughter) and their family's discussion and silence about the case that sent her grandmother to prison.

Primary sources on the people involved are the recorded facts in muster rolls, birth and death certificates, census data and newspaper accounts. To know the personalities of these people, I had to rely on their relatives who knew them in later years. From the documented facts, concreted in the ground like telephone poles, I needed to string a wire to connect one to the next. Dramatized scenes and dialog fill the questions between facts, based on intensive analysis of clues found in the journalistic reporting of the trial's testimony and family interviews.

Gay Leonard said to me early on in the research, "You know more about Jimmy Newton than anyone on Earth." Jimmy's parents and sister have passed, as has everyone who knew him personally. That statement hit my sense of responsibility to this World War II veteran's life and death. My goal is to treat Jimmy and Helen and the other people in their story with integrity and accuracy.

ACKNOWLEDGEMENTS

The murder and trial took place a block in each direction from my home—the Clark home to the east, the Washington County Courthouse to the west. Eighty years have passed since the murder of Jimmy Newton and the trial of Helen Clark. No one who participated in either is still alive.

Gay Leonard is the daughter of Dorothy Clark Leonard, the eldest daughter of Hal and Helen Clark.

Gay is the first grandchild of Helen Clark, and she lived her early years with her grandmother while her mother and father were first married. They later moved away, and Gay attended school in another county. She explained that some of the cousins knew nothing about the murder or trial. Helen's other daughters married and left the area. Dorothy came back to Abingdon. Yet no one in the family ever talked about Helen serving time in jail for murder. Gay had returned home from college before she knew about it. The family only told Dorothy's daughters then because Eva, the youngest daughter of Dorothy, was to attend elementary school in Abingdon. Dorothy was concerned another child would tell Eva that her grandmother had been in prison.

As a young adult, Gay asked questions of her mother, Dorothy, and tried to ask her grandmother. Dorothy revealed some details and her own belief of what happened. Helen, the grandmother, dismissed any talk of it.

PARTIAL LIST OF SOURCES

- Gay Leonard, the granddaughter of Helen Clark.
- Eva Leonard, the granddaughter of Helen Clark.
- Historical Society of Washington County, Virginia: newspapers, photographs and histories.
- Washington County Virginia Court records: court file (no transcripts exist); Patricia S. Moore, clerk of court; and Kathy Morefield.
- Washington County Virginia Public Library: Molly Schock, library director.
- Daytona Beach Florida Regional Library: Kim Dolce, local history librarian.
- Newspaper Archives: news coverage locally and nationwide.
- Primary documents for the Clark, Talbert, Newton, Smyth and Summers families
- Major General Rodney D. Fogg, (retired) U.S. Army.

1

THE MURDER

Rumors still circulate, eighty years later.

She left him dying upstairs and went to a movie.
There was no blood from the gunshots, the holes were plugged with paraffin.
He messed with the daughters; the mother took her revenge.
He was shot somewhere else, and the killer carried him into the house.
He was like a son to her.
She had romantic feelings for him.
He planned to abandon her.
She covered for the real murderer.
He pulled the trigger—suicide.
She pulled the trigger—murder.

A December snowstorm stranded Jimmy Newton in Abingdon, Virginia, in 1944. He boarded with a widow and her three daughters. Less than a year later, he was found dead of gunshot wounds on the floor of his rented room. The widow told several different stories to the sheriff. Eventually, she showed the sheriff where she hid the gun.

Mrs. Clark's trial made national news in the spring of 1946.

Helen Clark, a forty-four-year-old Gold Star mother and widow of a respected town council member and businessman, shot and left for dead Jimmy Newton, a twenty-two-year-old marine veteran of Guadalcanal and high school coach.

JIMMY NEWTON WALKED ALONG Valley Street with the milky November sun low in the sky. His earlier glass of bourbon leveled the pain in his hip. Sunday school had been well attended, and now, the afternoon service needed him as an altar assistant. Chief John Baden liked Jimmy; marines watched out for each other. At Pecan Street, Jimmy crossed over to Main Street and walked past the Presbyterian church to Saint Thomas Episcopal next door. Chief Baden served as the lay reader in the afternoon, a service for the many elderly congregants who didn't like the morning cold of attending early worship.

That past Friday morning, Jimmy and a pal had sat in a duck blind for a few hours, mostly drinking and talking. They'd shot at a few mallards, but really, Jimmy just wanted some male companionship. Living with Helen and the girls was swell. He had good food and a clean house, mostly provided by the daughters, Dorothy, Nancy and Frances. Mrs. Clark, or Helen, as she wanted to be called, spent little time cooking and cleaning. She had fallen into the blues; she was a widow facing the second anniversary of her son, Hal Jr., being killed in Bougainville in the Pacific.

God, how many of Jimmy's friends had died in the Pacific? His best friend, Clarke Beetlestone, had gone missing in action (MIA) a year ago. Word made it back to the States that "Beet" was assumed dead. Their plans, made shoulder to shoulder in the jungle of Guadalcanal, would never come about. He wiped his eyes as he entered the church.

November was a shit month. Beet had gone MIA last November and was definitely dead. Hal Jr. had been killed in the Solomon Islands two Novembers ago. Jimmy knew that if he hadn't been injured on a transport ship in October 1942, he wouldn't have made it to that November.

The aroma of woody incense calmed Jimmy as he stepped into the narthex. A deep breath, then another. He entered the sanctuary, and Chief Baden motioned him up the lectern. Jimmy smoothed his hair as he walked up the red carpeted aisle. "Jim, glad you could help this afternoon," Chief Baden said as he shook Jimmy's hand in a firm and long grip—as a father would. "You going to see your folks in Kentucky?"

"Tuesday," Jimmy said. "We have a Thanksgiving morning hunting trip planned." The urge for a swig of bourbon wrapped around Jimmy's thoughts—something to calm his nerves, a taste to take the edge off his physical pain. Maybe—if he would admit it to himself—it would ease his emotional pain, too.

He had a flask in his jacket pocket.

He excused himself to get the altar prepared with the communion plate and chalice. The wine smelled sweet and inviting. His hands trembled, knocking over the handbell. The bells and smells of the Episcopal church soothed him—if he could just stop the stabbing pain in his hip and leg. Jimmy slipped out the back door of the church to smoke a Lucky Strike and have a few swallows of bourbon. He would be singing in the choir this afternoon, and the Luckies and juice oiled his cords. A few more swigs. He chuckled. The chronic pain had backed away to a dull throb.

⬥

HELEN SAT IN THE rocking chair next to her parlor fireplace. Her older daughters Dorothy and Nancy chattered in the kitchen as they prepared Sunday supper. She could smell the tang of chicken searing in the pan. Nancy argued with Dorothy about how doughy the dumplings should be. Dorothy, at seventeen, reminded Helen of herself at that age—at least looks-wise. Blond and naturally beautiful, she attracted the attention of every man she met, no matter how young or old. Toddler boys gravitated to Dorothy. Old men walked straighter and sucked in their bellies around her. But her manner was the opposite of Helen's at her age. Dorothy was a tomboy. She had followed her father and brother everywhere. She could shoot a gun better than most men in the county. She spent her free time at the filling station, working on automobiles. As for dresses and jewelry, Dorothy had the best, but she preferred her work trousers or, heaven forbid, those canvas coveralls. Nancy acted more girlish—maybe because she was a year younger than Dorothy and was exposed to her older sister's femininity, no matter the roughness of Dorothy's manner at times. Nancy was tough in her intellect, smart like her Grandmother Talbert. Then there was Frances, the youngest, who was almost nine years old. The loss of her father and brother hadn't injured Frances as it had Dorothy. Frances was barely more than four when her father died. Her recollection of Hal Clark must have been vague at best.

Helen could sense the walls bearing in on her. She had turned forty-four the month before. Her hair had strands of gray. She should go to the beauty parlor. Her depression had lifted with the arrival of Jimmy. She would plan a celebration of the one year anniversary of his coming to Abingdon. What sunshine that young man had brought with him. Although, he had his demons, too. His war injury plagued him. His wounded hip and agonizing headaches left him incapacitated at times. She knew he took to drink to ease

13

the pain. He was a particular boy, in that his affections toward Helen and the girls would run warm and then suddenly cold. Someone or something called to him from the shadows of his life. Helen understood that.

Frances pulled plates from the china cabinet and set the table for the five of them.

Helen pushed herself up from the rocking chair. "Dorothy, will Jack be joining us for supper?" Jack Henderson was Dorothy's current boyfriend. Dorothy came to the kitchen doorway. At least she's wearing a dress, Helen thought. Dorothy said Jack would not dine with them and that he'd be arriving later to drive them to the movie theater. "So, it's just the family tonight," Helen said as she helped Frances place the plates.

A few minutes later, Jimmy strolled in, whistling the Andrew Sisters' "Rum and Coca-Cola" tune. He was as big as her late husband, Hal, probably six feet tall, but thinner. Jimmy washed up in the kitchen, and then they sat down for supper.

Conversation flowed around who had attended the church service and about going to the late movie. Dorothy didn't want Jack to get the impression they were going steady. That was why she'd invited her mother, sisters and Jimmy to come along to the Cameo Theater.

The girls cleared the table after everyone finished. Jimmy walked out to the porch to smoke a cigarette. Helen went to her room upstairs to change for the outing.

She heard male voices on the sidewalk and peeked out her front bedroom window to see some of Jimmy's students from Damascus motioning him over to their car. Jimmy coached the boys in football, and they followed him around like puppies. The boy in the front passenger seat got out and climbed in the back. Jimmy took the front seat next to the driver, and the car drove off. The departing automobile caused Helen to huff with frustration. He knows we're leaving soon for the show, she thought.

After about fifteen minutes, the car returned. Jimmy and the three boys from Damascus High School remained in the automobile. The sun had set, and the evening had grown chilly.

Jack Henderson arrived in a cab, stopped by the boys' car and talked briefly with Jimmy. He came into the house, greeting Dorothy and her sisters. Helen left her bedroom, ready for the movie in Bristol. Jack explained they were going to the Cameo to see Burgess Meredith in the *Story of G.I. Joe*.

Helen glanced out the parlor window and saw that Jimmy was still in the car with the boys. She went to the front porch and stood. No one acknowledged her. She marched down the steps and to the passenger side of the car, where Jimmy sat. "Are you going to the show or not?" she asked him. He looked at the boys and smiled. She didn't have time for his immaturity. "Give me the keys to our car."

He pulled the keys from his pocket and dangled them out the window. She grabbed them and went back up to the porch. She could hear the boys stifling laughs. She slammed the front door as she entered the foyer.

Nancy jerked her head around at the commotion. Dorothy exhaled slowly and asked Jack to go see if Jimmy was going with them. Helen handed Jack the car keys as he walked by her. When he reached to open the door, Jimmy and the three Damascus boys entered, and the boys joined the girls in the parlor.

Helen and Jimmy spoke in hushed tones in the foyer, away from the teenagers.

"Guess we better chop chop so y'all can get to the show," one of the boys said. The girls and Jack grabbed their coats while the Damascus boys headed out the door and back down to their car. Jimmy followed them out.

Jimmy stood by the gate. Dorothy, Jack and Frances propped themselves against their car's fender, waiting. Helen and Nancy remained on the porch at the front door. Helen called out, "Bring me my coat."

No one answered. She raised her eyebrow as she looked at Jimmy by the sidewalk gate. "I never get your coat," he said as he turned toward the boys in their car.

"Jackass," Helen said. He's maddening, she thought, especially around those boys. He's the man of the house and should act like it. Nancy sighed and went inside to get her mother's coat. With a huff, Helen went back into the house, and little Frances ran up the steps and followed her mother inside as well.

The boys started their car, and Jimmy said his goodbyes. He returned to the house.

Jack and Dorothy leaned against the side of the car, waiting to see who was going with them. Jack checked his watch: 8:20 p.m. They would have to leave soon to make the show.

The front door opened, and Nancy and Frances came out and walked down the steps to the car. "Let's go. Mother isn't going, and Jimmy has other plans," Nancy told them.

Jack drove the girls west on Valley Street and south on Court Street to get to Main Street. At the corner of Court and Main Streets, they saw the Damascus boys drive by and wave to them. The boys later said the time was 8:25 p.m., and they noticed that Jimmy and Mrs. Clark were not in the car with the Clark daughters.

THE HOUSE AT 407 East Valley Street held the November darkness around it like a cloak. An occasional car drove past. To the west of the home, a large lawn with trees and an evergreen hedge spread next to the neighbor's property. To the east, the L.P. Summers's home was empty.

At the Clark house, the back upstairs bedroom had one window with a dim lamp on. No one was around to see or hear. Flashes sparked and lit up the windowpanes, with one blast, two—three and four.

Silence settled on the house.

A moment later, the front door opened. Helen Clark walked down the steps to the sidewalk. She went next door to the Summerses's house.

Returning to her own home, she grabbed her purse and coat and then locked the front door behind her. She hesitated with the house key in her hand but then dropped it into her purse. She walked down the porch steps to the sidewalk gate and then turned west along Valley Street.

At the intersection of Pecan Street, she crossed to Main Street and kept walking. A block away, in front of the Methodist church, she saw a couple of Dorothy's schoolmates. There was one boy—she couldn't remember his name—who nodded to her. "She seemed out of breath, as though she had been walking fast, and asked us to take her to Bristol, saying her girls had gone off and left her," Billy Vance would later testify. "But we decided we couldn't go."

With the schoolboys of no help, Helen continued to her destination. On Wall Street, next to the bus station, she inquired at the taxi stand for a ride to Bristol. Martin Mitchell, the cab driver, described to the jury that they left Abingdon around 9:00 p.m. and arrived at the Cameo Theater in Bristol at 9:30 p.m.

Helen paid for her movie ticket and entered the dark theater. She saw her daughters and slipped into the row behind them. Once the picture ended, she joined her daughters and Jack Henderson on their drive back to Abingdon, returning at 11:30 p.m.

Jack and the girls, along with Helen, talked for a while in the parlor. Helen, Nancy and Frances excused themselves to go to bed. They all walked by Jimmy's bedroom door on their way to the bathroom that evening. Before retiring to her front bedroom, Helen called down to Dorothy and Jack to leave the front door unlocked so Jimmy could get in.

With the cold sunrise on Monday, November 19, Helen Clark went downstairs, picked up the newspaper from the front porch and lit the heater.

BRISTOL HERALD COURIER, BRISTOL, VIRGINIA-TENNE

WHERE NEWTON WAS FATALLY SHOT

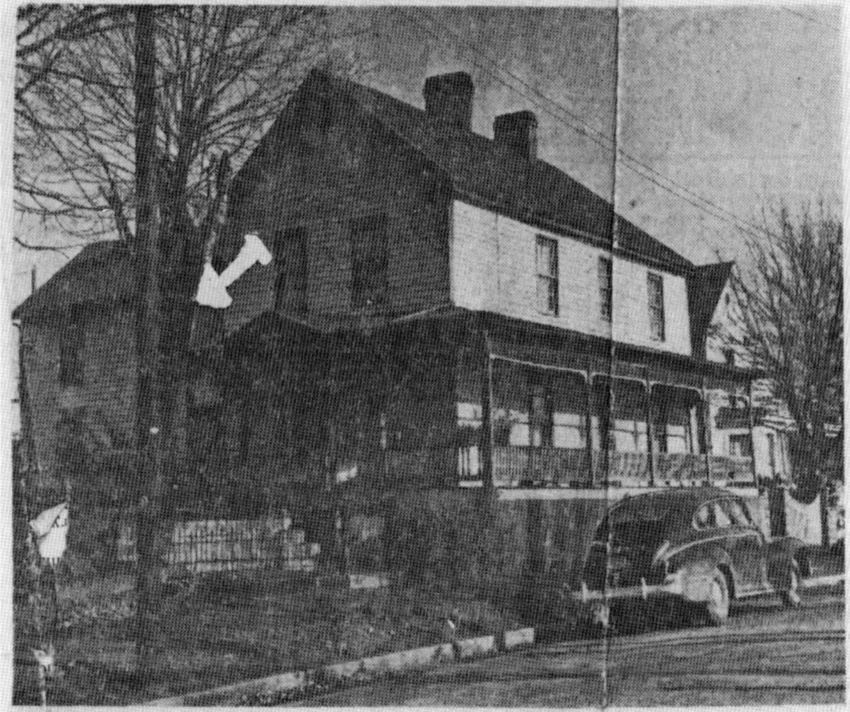

Pictured above is the Valley street "death house" in Abingdon, Va., where James Emmett Newton, III, 22, was found dead Monday morning, by his own hand, so Sheriff J. Trigg Woodward quoted Mrs. Hal V. Clark, 44, his landlady; murdered, according to Commonwealth's Attorney Roby C. Thompson who has obtained a warrant naming Mrs. Clark as his slayer. The two windows on the side of the house, with drawn shades, look into Mrs. Clark's room. The window back of the ell-shaped front, partly obscured by the corner of the porch and tree limbs, marks the room in which the body of Newton, popular teacher and football coach at Damascus, Va., was found on the floor bearing four bullet wounds.

A newspaper photograph of the boardinghouse. The arrow indicates Jimmy's room on the second floor. *From the* Bristol *(TN)* Herald Courier.

At 7:30 a.m., the girls stirred upstairs, and Helen called to sixteen-year-old Nancy to wake up Jimmy so he wouldn't be late getting to Damascus.

She waited in the parlor.

Nancy came rushing down the stairs with Dorothy behind her. "We think Jimmy is dead," Nancy said.

"Mother, he's cold—on the floor." Dorothy scanned the parlor for Frances. She didn't want her young sister to overhear.

Helen sat still for a moment, not looking at her daughters. All she said was, "Call your Uncle C."

C.M. Talbert, Helen's brother, came with a Black man, Louis Goins, who drove for a local butcher. C.M. went upstairs to Jimmy's room. He asked Louis to stay at the sidewalk. About eight minutes later, C.M. called down for Louis to come in. Jimmy lay on the floor by his bed, fully clothed, including his sports jacket. They saw no blood. Louis picked up one of Jimmy's hands and realized he was dead.

C.M. and Louis came down to Helen to report that Jimmy was indeed dead. Helen told them to call the doctor. Louis suggested the undertaker was a better idea.

The undertaker arrived and took Jimmy's body to the funeral home and called the sheriff. With the physical examination of the body, the undertaker and coroner found four bullet wounds, two in Jimmy's chest and two in his back.

Helen's narrative of the event changed several times while talking with the sheriff and the commonwealth's attorney.

Thirty-six hours after the discovery of Jimmy's lifeless body, Helen Clark was charged with murder. One of the most scandalous trials of the region began.

2

VISTA ELLEN "HELEN" TALBERT CLARK

Vista Ellen "Helen" Talbert was the seventh of eight children to Charles "Charley" Matthew Talbert and Frances "Fannie" Elizabeth Davis Talbert. Both Charley and Fannie grew up on farms in Washington County, Virginia.

The Davis family worked hard and sent their eldest daughter, Fannie, to Martha Washington College. The college was the social center of Abingdon for young people. Dances, theater productions and countryside outings brought the "Martha girls" into the community. Fannie met girls from up and down the East Coast of the United States. She was a local girl, and at one of these social events, she met local boy Charley Talbert.

Fannie graduated from Martha Washington College in 1883. Then she and Charley were married on March 3, 1885. She furthered her education at Radford State Teachers College. For the next twenty years, Fannie and Charley had eight children. Fannie taught in Washington County, Virginia public schools for thirty-nine years. Historian and writer Jane Douglas Summers Brown said Fannie was "my beloved Sunday school teacher during my teen years." Ms. Summers Brown touted, "She [Mrs. Talbert] was a graduate of Martha Washington College." Her degree was a rare achievement for a local girl in the 1880s.

The 1900 census listed Charley and Fannie living on a rented farm in Washington County. Their sons Robert (thirteen), James (eleven) and John (eight) attended school. Frank (six), Willie (four) and Effie (two) were at home. Vista Ellen "Helen" Talbert was born on Thursday, October 3, 1901, in Alum Wells, off Rich Valley Road.

Charley and Fannie moved their family to the farm of Captain Francis Smith Robertson, called "Mary's Meadows." Mary's Meadows consisted of thousands of acres. The large farm was a result of the marriage of two prominent families: Francis Smith III and Mary Frances Trigg King, the recent widow of William King. Their daughter was Mary Trigg Smith, for whom the farm was named.

Mary Trigg Smith married Governor Wyndham Robertson, a descendant of Pocahontas and John Rolfe. Mary Trigg Smith and Governor Wyndham Robertson were the parents of Captain Francis Smith Robertson, the man who hired the Talberts to come help run his farm.

The Talbert family had all boys until Effie was born. Robert, the oldest, was twelve and acted as a junior father to baby Effie. She became a toddler who got into mischief, so Robert's affections quickly turned to Helen when she arrived in the fall of 1901. A new baby girl, sparkling eyes and blond curls, captured all the brothers' hearts.

"Baby sister," Robert whispered to the infant Helen while he watched the sun set from a rocker on their front porch, "no one will ever hurt you. No man will break your heart. You have brothers who will always be around. You'll be safe and loved." He would make sure his sisters had all they could ever wish for.

His brothers James, John and Frank called from the farm's lower pasture. "Gig time!" The lure of twilight frog gigging won out over rocking his baby sister to sleep. Robert went inside and handed the baby to his mother. "Heading to the creek." She held the baby tight and managed to holler to Robert before he jumped off the porch, "You and your brothers take off your boots before getting in that creek!"

As the years ticked along, another son, C.M., came five years after Helen. The older boys took odd jobs along with their farm work to help the large family. But the odd jobs didn't bring in enough money for Robert's liking. Now in his mid-twenties, Robert found financial stability to be a driving force. The Virginia-Carolina Railway Company needed strong, young men. Loaded with timber from the forests of Damascus and Whitetop, the "Virginia Creeper" line creeped down the steep rails to Abingdon. Switching the loaded cars to move the timber along to mills required manpower, and Robert Talbert saw the opportunity. The railway company hired him on the spot. He started apprenticing with one of the experienced brakemen.

That evening, Robert rushed home to tell his parents, brothers and sisters of his new job. Finally, he would make enough money to move into his own place, maybe starting by renting a room near the depot.

The news caught twelve-year-old Helen off-guard. Robert was her hero, her protector. He will spend his life with us, she thought. We can all live on this farm. The prospect of the brothers creating families of their own hadn't really occurred to Helen. Like a lot of adolescent girls, her world revolved around her.

Robert noticed the frown on Helen's face and watched her stomp out the door and to the porch. He followed. "Baby girl, I'm not going anywhere just yet. I'm ready to see the countryside. Imagine riding that train, standing on top of a car with the wind on your face; the fields smell of fresh cut hay and cattle; the woods full of deer galloping along the tracks; rivers with fish jumping and kids playing—all laid out in front of you. I'm excited."

"You'll leave me," she said and turned away from him.

He plopped down on a rocking chair and pulled her to his knee. "You are my girl. Don't tell Effie, but you're my favorite." He grinned when she laughed. "That train makes round trips every day. It ain't taking me to distant lands—just up to Whitetop and back. I'll be home every night."

This satisfied Helen for the moment. "Promise you won't leave me."

"You're always a part of me," he said.

She knew he hadn't made the promise she wanted.

Robert's new job entailed dangerous manual labor. A brakeman's tasks consisted of climbing up and along the top of a moving train car when the engineer signaled for brakes. Robert would turn the brake wheel to apply the brakes to his assigned cars. With the steep grade of the line from Whitetop Mountain to Abingdon, brakemen had to manage multiple cars' brakes to keep the train at a safe speed. The speed may have been the only safe aspect of the train. Robert also coupled and uncoupled cars from each other while the train moved, slowly along a sidetrack. Brakemen did the switching of the tracks, as well. At the Abingdon depot, a sidetrack was used to juggle the cars, leaving some at the freight depot for loading and unloading and to be picked up later by the engine.

A few weeks in, Robert kept developing his brakeman skills. He climbed to the roof of the first car in the line that needed to be routed to the sidetracks. Several cars of timber rolled from the main line and stopped at the freight yard. The tricky maneuver required Robert to uncouple the first timber freight car from the moving train to allow the orphaned cars to slow. As the engine and its connected cars moved on, Robert jumped down to outrun the coasting orphans and pulled the switch to move the rails to the sidetracks so the timber cars rolled parallel to the main line and stopped at the depot.

He had executed this maneuver several times. That April morning, the cable that operated the rail switch got caught, and the rails almost didn't transfer to the sidetracks. He had managed to loosen the cable and successfully transfer the cars. He hopped aboard the train heading back up the mountain for the next circuit.

After 5:00 p.m., Robert rode the last train of the day with cars to be disengaged as it rounded from the Creeper line to the depot. Robert and other brakemen climbed up to help the engine slow the train cars as they neared the freight yard and its parallel rails. The smell of cattle hung in the air from the last train that must have pulled out an hour before.

The junction came into view.

He uncoupled the lead car in the line to be orphaned and jumped to the ground. His boots crunched on the gravel as he jogged along the tracks to the switch.

The switch wouldn't move. He pulled with all his strength. The uncoupled line of rail cars rolled toward the junction. Robert jerked at the lever, and then it occurred to him that the cable needed to be loosened, just as he had fixed it that morning.

He braced his boot against the edge of the rail and pulled the wire cable so he could adjust its tension.

The cable snapped.

The recoil caught Robert in the chest and knocked him to the rail.

Abingdon freight depot, 1920. *Author's collection.*

The line of freight cars clunked toward him.

Men yelled and rushed to the rails.

The steel wheels rolled quickly.

A scream sliced the air.

The freight cars' wheels cleaved Robert's body, completely severing his left leg at the thigh and cutting off his left arm and shoulder.

The *Washington County Journal* reported that Robert was "almost instantly killed." Later in the article, the reporter added, "He is not known to have spoken a word but lived in this condition about ten minutes."

Those ten minutes were not enough time to notify Charley or Fannie about their oldest son's condition or for them to be with him in his last moments. He died with his railroad crew around him.

Helen, then only twelve years old, gathered with her parents, siblings and extended family members and friends at Sinking Spring Cemetery, within view of the freight station, for Robert's funeral. On the northern side of the hill, Robert was laid to rest. He shared an obelisk marker with his grandfather Isaac Davis. Lilacs, snapdragon and lily-of-the-valley blanketed the base of the headstone. The morning breeze floated the scents of the flowers through the cemetery. Robert's brothers tried to remain stoic, but eight-year-old C.M. huddled with Effie in grief. Fannie sat in a wooden chair and stared toward the railroad in the distance. Charley stood behind Fannie, one hand on her shoulder and his other hand trembling by his side.

Charley's brother nodded to Charley and hooked his head toward a sheltering pine a few paces away. Charley stepped back, and they shared a few swigs of emotion-stunting whiskey.

Helen couldn't cry. How could Robert be stolen from her? Grief hovered, but anger brewed in her heart. She wanted to scream, claw at the ground, curse God and the preacher who droned on without anyone listening or caring about what he said. Robert was gone.

Helen heard it first. Her head snapped toward the train tracks. An engine blew

Robert Talbert's gravestone in Sinking Spring Cemetery. *Author's collection.*

Teenage Vista Ellen "Helen" Talbert. *Eva Leonard.*

its horn as it traveled the rails—a painful, melancholy wail. Churning wheels squeaked as the train slowed. She felt as if the sound slashed her heart. Her inhale brought no breath but let loose tears, convulsing, shuddering. The slope of the hill seemed to move. Her brother John grabbed her in his arms before she dropped to her knees.

Weeks passed before Helen returned to school. She and C.M. were the only siblings still attending classes. Fannie had encouraged the older children to continue their education, but as they trudged through high school, one by one, they quit going and took jobs.

A lovely child, Helen grew into a beautiful young girl. Historian and writer Jane Douglas Summers Brown said Helen "was a blonde, tall, slender and attractive. As a young girl she was very pretty. We were classmates at William King High School."

Helen's brother John, despite worry from his mother and sisters, worked with the railway. As a fireman, he shoveled coal into the firebox of the train's boiler to produce the steam to run the train. This was hard work, but it was not as dangerous as Robert's brakeman tasks. Also, the fireman acted as the engineer-in-training, a prime position for a young man.

As tensions grew in Europe, some local men moved to Hopewell, Virginia, just outside Richmond. DuPont Company's guncotton plant needed workers. Guncotton was a replacement for gunpowder in weapons. John Talbert and Hal Clark, both from Abingdon, worked in Hopewell around 1916.

In April 1917, the United States declared war on Germany. John continued working for the war effort with DuPont. Hal Clark left the DuPont plant and came back to Abingdon to register for the draft.

Because of his wartime work, John Talbert was exempted from the draft and stayed in touch with his parents and younger siblings at home. John sent Helen gifts from Richmond. He mailed her clothes from stores like Thalhimers and Miller and Rhoads. She was the best-dressed girl at William King High School. "Oh, this dress?" she would say when asked by classmates (her granddaughter Gay later retold). "My brother John had that sent to me from Richmond."

While John worked at DuPont, his brothers James, Frank and William served in the military. They returned from Europe in the summer of 1919.

HAL CLARK

After World War I, Hal Clark returned from France and arrived in Boston on July 4, 1919, aboard the White Star Line's SS *Vedic*. He was in Company A, 534 Engineers Service Battalion, where he served as a sergeant of engineers.

Twenty-six-year-old Hal J. Clark was born in Abingdon in 1893 to James Thomas Clark and Mary Ellen Campbell Clark.

Hal's 1917 draft card lists him as a twenty-four-year-old farmer, single, tall and medium build, with brown eyes and brown hair. The year after he returned from France, the 1920 census listed Hal as a fireman on a locomotive. Like Helen's brother John, Hal Clark saw this position as a step toward becoming a train engineer.

The Presbyterian church in Abingdon, then and now, is Sinking Spring Presbyterian Church. James and Mary Ellen Clark, regular parishioners at Sinking Spring, raised their children in the church, as did Charley and Fannie Talbert. The Talberts and the Clarks had children of similar ages. Helen's brother John had returned from the Richmond area and his job with Dupont, and he resumed his railroad work as a fireman.

John's coworker at DuPont and again on the railroad and fellow Presbyterian Hal Clark, age twenty-six, would usually occupy the same pew as John and the other young bachelors of the church. As war veterans, these men were ready to settle down and start families. John invited Effie to sit in the pew in front of the young men, so she did. But she brought along her eighteen-year-old sister, Helen.

Hal Clark complimented Helen on her singing of the hymns and asked if he could call on her. Hal's sister Rachel was a year older than Helen. His other sister, Lucy Gay, was fourteen. The Clark girls had attended school with Helen. Rachel, Lucy Gay and Hal's mother, Mary Ellen, were not excited by the prospect of Hal courting a Talbert girl.

The Clarks owned their large farm. The Talberts managed a farm not of their ownership. Mrs. Talbert, or "Fannie," was a well-respected Sunday school teacher and public school teacher. John Talbert and Hal Clark were coworkers on the railroad. Yet, in terms of their station in life in the 1920s, Abingdon set the Talberts at a different level than the highly regarded Clarks.

In a *Romeo and Juliet*–type relationship, Hal Clark fell in love with the stunning Helen Talbert. Helen was one of the most beautiful girls in town, and Hal was the most promising of the eligible bachelors.

"My grandfather was besotted," Gay Leonard described. "He was head over heels in love."

Hal's mother and sisters didn't feel that Helen had the appropriate standing in Abingdon society that a wife of young Hal Clark should possess. "His family thought she wasn't good enough for him. But they would have thought that nobody was good enough for him, because he'd been in the war when the U.S. soldiers kicked the Germans' asses. Plus, he drove the train," Gay added.

Helen had talents that she didn't flaunt, mainly because her looks were valued more than her mind. "She could look at a column of figures and tell you the total," Gay said. "Crazy as a damn loon and brilliant." Being one of the town beauties, Helen had become accustomed to getting what she wanted.

And she wanted Hal Clark.

Charismatic and charming—when he wanted to be—Hal Clark drew people to him. His days were filled with invitations to picnics, dances, ball games, hunting trips, skeet shooting contests and horse shows and riding competitions. Helen Talbert was always by his side.

John mentioned to his sister that Hal was a favorite of the management of the Virginia-Carolina Railway Company. The Virginia-Carolina Railway

Company merged with Norfolk and Western. The new management promoted Hal to engineer and assigned him to engineer long-haul and passenger trains. Frequent trips to New York introduced Hal to people from all over the East Coast. He had always enjoyed equestrian sports, and to interact with horse trainers, jockeys and even horse owners thrilled young Hal.

Hal met wealthy and famous people during those train engineering days. While on routes, especially when he was going into the flatlands of the Carolinas and Georgia piedmont, Hal let his engineer assistant take the controls as he talked with the passengers in the dining and Pullman cars. His interest in horses led him to the equine-based society of southern stables, competitions and racetracks.

Hal became friends with the men who managed the stables of Woolworth heiress Barbara Hutton on her plantation south of Charleston, South Carolina. "My grandfather [Hal] and Little Hal liked to hunt quail and grouse with Johnny Phillips, the young horse trainer, at the Hutton Plantation," Gay said. In later years, Hal took Helen and their children to stay at the thirty-five-room plantation house. He would also bring his English setter birddogs so he and his son could hunt.

HAL AND HELEN

Hal and Helen Clark lived an extended romance. *Eva Leonard.*

On September 30, 1922, Hal Clark married Helen Talbert. He was twenty-nine and she was twenty. They moved to a small house on Main Street on the east side of Courthouse Hill.

Nine months later, Hal Jr. was born on June 29, 1923.

Helen convinced Hal to give up the railway life. The memory of her brother Robert's death always shadowed her emotions as Hal boarded the train. With the arrival of their son, Helen wanted Hal close to home. Hal started an electrical contracting company.

On March 19, 1928, Hal and Helen welcomed their first daughter, Dorothy Ellen Clark. Five-year-old Hal Jr. had a new playmate and companion.

HELEN'S BROTHER FRANK HAD been fighting a cough since he went into the military for World War I. He enlisted at Camp Humphrey, Virginia, but was discharged three months later. He had consumption. Pulmonary tuberculosis (TB), or consumption, as it was commonly called, began with a cough that continued for months. The disease progressed to include intermittent fevers. Frank became fatigued, thin and pale—as if he was being consumed by the TB virus. His labored breathing shot sharp pains through his chest. His injured lungs produced blood that he coughed up, causing more pain and agony. For Frank, this lasted ten years. The handsome, tall, blue-gray-eyed and sandy blond–haired twenty-four-year-old soldier who went into the military in 1918 was bedridden at his parents' home by June 1928.

His cough rattled the quiet of the house. Fannie placed a cool washrag on Frank's throat. The strong young man was wasting away, and his mother felt powerless to ease his pain.

"Mother," Helen called from the front door.

Fannie left Frank in his room and met Helen in the parlor. "You get on out on the porch," Fannie said. "Keep those babies safe from the consumption. And yourself."

"But, Mother, what about you and Papa?"

"Don't worry about us. We've made it this long. I'll bring Frank out on the porch, and you can talk to him there."

Back in Frank's room, Fannie struggled to sit him upright and slide him from the bed to his chair. Charley had nailed the chair to a board with wheels. Frank tried to push himself, but Fannie could tell her son's weakness overcame his effort. So, he finally allowed his mother to move him.

"Sorry, Mama," he said in a raspy voice.

"No need to apologize to me. We are in this together."

Moving him that day was easier than it had been the day before. Fannie couldn't tell if she was getting stronger or if Frank weighed less—probably both.

"The sun is bright and warm. That will feel good on your body. Fresh air always does you well." Fannie tried to sell the effort and reward of getting to the porch. "Plus, Helen is waiting out there to see you."

Frank grinned. Fannie knew Frank loved to hear about his little nephew and baby niece. She rolled the chair to a sunny spot on the porch, across from where Helen perched on the railing, about ten feet away.

"You look very pretty today," Fannie complimented her daughter.

"Thank you. Hal wants us to go to the Hutton Plantation for a few weeks. He's ready for some hunting and skeet shooting with his friends down there." Helen looked to her mother for the question Fannie knew she was really asking but didn't want to say in front of Frank.

"That sounds fine. Frank and I will keep things running here until you get back."

A slight exhale from Helen signaled that she understood Fannie expected Frank to still be alive by the time Hal, Helen and the children returned to Abingdon. "Let me tell you what mischief Little Hal got himself into," Helen began with a chipper voice.

"He's a rascal," Frank said low and hoarse.

Fannie turned and went into the house and to the kitchen.

By the end of December 1928, Frank's skeletal body could barely breathe without causing cough spasms and choking on blood. He passed away on December 30.

"I CAN'T, I JUST can't take anymore death." Helen stood in the backyard of their little house on Main Street.

Hal had worried about Helen's nervousness. Their children's constant craving for her attention; her brothers Robert and Frank's deaths; his sisters' lack of civility toward her; her father's drinking; her mother's selfless attention to everyone except herself; it all weighed heavy on Helen. He could see the strain on her face.

"And this house," she said. "We need a larger home for our family."

"We'll find a place." He turned to go back into the house but realized she hadn't budged. "Get inside. It's too cold for you to be out here."

"Hal, we need a larger house by the end of summer."

"What's the hurry?"

She placed her hands on her stomach. "Another baby."

LATE IN THE SPRING of 1929, the Rye Cove tornado hit Scott County, about sixty miles west of Abingdon. At 12:55 p.m., a tornado raced up a plateau in Rye Cove where the school sat. The children were in their classrooms just after their midday recess.

Principal A.B. Nolan described the sighting, "I was walking through the hall when I saw what looked like a whirlwind coming up the hollow. Trees were swaying. As it neared the school building, it became a black cloud; it appeared as though a tremendous amount of dirt had been gathered. I think I yelled. It struck the building. The next thing I remembered I was standing knee deep in a pond seventy-five feet from where the building stood before it was demolished."

Student John Runyon, seventeen, and teacher Elizabeth Richmond were standing by a classroom window when they saw the tornado. John said he noticed the trees swaying violently. "It just picked up the schoolhouse. The next thing I know, I had about half of it on me and was trying to dig out." There were about 155 children in the school at the time. Many injured students and faculty members were taken to regional hospitals. Twelve students, aged six to eighteen, died. One teacher, Mary Ava Carter, twenty-four years old and the first grade teacher, was killed.

Hal Clark jumped into action, assisting to replace the school—the only school in that region for many miles. Hal and his electrical services company wired the new school and kept to the schedule to have the Rye Cove Memorial High School open in the fall of 1930.

Aftermath of the Rye Cove tornado in 1929 that demolished the Scott County, Virginia, school. *Library of Virginia.*

Hal and Helen Clark's home on East Valley Street. *Author's collection.*

While Hal began working in Scott County to replace Rye Cove School, Helen gave birth to their second daughter, Nancy Barney Clark, on August 24, 1929.

The 1930 census listed Hal and Helen Clark living at 407 East Valley Street. This two-story home had a grand stairway at its entrance, four bedrooms, a bath upstairs, a parlor, a dining room and a kitchen.

Known as the Jacob Clark House, the Clarks' home was one of the oldest in Abingdon, since it included the 1825 log house of Jacob Clark. Jane Douglas Summers Brown wrote: "To its west lay a very large lawn with a vegetable garden and apple orchard in the rear….The house sits on a high brick foundation immediately on the sidewalk. The western portion of the lot was enclosed by a paling fence but as it neared the house it became iron leading to the entrance." Ms. Summers Brown listed previous owners over the years, including Benjamin Clark, W.W. Clark (Hal's grandfather), James Betts and James H. Hines (Abingdon's mayor, 1893–1911 and 1930–31. James H. Hines was Hal's uncle, married to his aunt Millie Gay Clark).

After the Rye Cove School was completed, Hal opened an additional business. In 1931, he and R.C. Ropp bought the corner lot at East Main and Tanner Streets. They removed the old house there and built a filling station. The Ropp and Clark Service Station consisted of fuel pumps and garage services. "My grandfather ran his electrical contracting business out of a big barn in the back of the service station," Gay Leonard described.

Have Beautiful
LAWNS

DON'T WORRY WITH A DULL LAWN MOWER

Send it to us and let us sharpen it on an automatic
Lawn Mower Sharpener. Precision sharpening and
adjusting of your mower assures perfect cutting.

Ropp & Clark

ELECTRICAL CONTRACTORS
S E R V I C E   S T A T I O N
East Main Street   Abingdon, Va.

A newspaper advertisement for the Ropp and Clark Service Station and Electrical Contractors, featuring Hal Clark with his children, (*left to right*) Hal Jr., Nancy and Dorothy. *Author's collection.*

Helen took care of Hal's home and children and supported him in his professional and social endeavors. In turn, Hal adored Helen. Even after having three children, the couple still took time for themselves. Dinner with friends, dances, trips to New York City, horse shows and races around the Southeast thrilled Helen. Hal's electrical contracting business and service station thrived. He was able to bestow expensive gifts on his beautiful, young wife.

Mr. and Mrs. Hal Clark dominated the social scene. "The family of Hal Clark stands out in my memory," Jane Douglas Summers Brown wrote. "Hal was a handsome, virile man, a hunter and a lover of horses. His sometimes roughness in manner and temper was sublimated by his innate kindness and friendly accommodation." Summers Brown added that Helen "was vivacious and high strung."

When Hal's uncle and town mayor James H. Hines died, Hal saw that the sudden loss had disrupted Abingdon leadership. Hal decided to run for town council. The 1932 council consisted of nine men. In order of the most

Hal J. Clark portrait. *Gay Leonard.*

votes received, the elected were: E.J. Clifton, T.C. Phillips, Dr. E.B. Denton, Hal Clark, J.F. Branson, Tom Hayter, W.H. Stiles, Dr. F.H. Moore and C.E. Smith. The elected mayor was R.B. Hagy.

Hal did not run for reelection in the next town council election in 1934. He developed his businesses, enjoyed his young family and pursued his interest in the outdoors. The family traveled frequently to Florida for equestrian events.

Hal brought Hal Jr. in to help with the filling station when Hal Jr. was twelve. "He, assisted by his young son, Hal," Jane Douglas Summers Brown wrote, "operated a gas station on the western corner of Main and Tanner Streets. His friend was Garnet Booker who lived at the 'Booker Place' [farm], later 'Winterham.'"

The January 18, 1935 edition of the *Bristol News Bulletin* reported, "Messrs. Hal Clark and G.Y. Booker left Monday for Younger [*sic*] Island, S.C. for a week's hunting trip." This location referred to Younge Island, south of Charleston, where Hal's friend Johnny Phillips worked at the Barbara Hutton Plantation. Johnny, like Hal and Garnet, was a horse enthusiast and sport hunter.

The 1936 election cycle for town council saw Hal Clark run. Once again, he was elected. "New members to council, elected on June 9: W.H. Stiles, E.J. Clifton, W.H. Perdue, E.B. Denton, J.W. Hutton, Hal Clark, Roger Warren, Dr. French H. Moore, Tom Hayter." The first meeting of the new council occurred in September 1936. Attorney Embree W. Potts, a former mayor, was "retained in the capacity of supervisor of the new Abingdon sewer project." Hal served on the Streets Committee and the Sewer Committee.

While Hal ran his businesses and worked with town council to improve Abingdon, Helen prepared for another baby. Their third daughter, Frances Evelyn Clark, was born on December 15, 1936.

Helen wasn't alone in caring for the four children. "Kathleen DeBose cooked and ran the house. She was my grandmother's housekeeper," Gay Leonard explained. "She was a beautiful Black lady. I knew her children, David 'Belasco' and Maggie. They told me about going with their mother to work and playing with mother [Dorothy] and Aunt Nancy. It's like Kathleen just took my grandmother's kids and she raised the little girls. My grandmother was an ornament. I don't think that's much of an exaggeration. Her job was to be beautiful and be ready to have fun when he [Hal] came home."

Hal and Helen led a life of an extended romance. The children, especially "Little Hal," as Hal Jr. was referred to, delighted their parents. But the focus of their relationship was on each other. "They would go out dancing at roadhouses," Gay Leonard said. "Kathleen took care of the children."

Hal and a delegation from the American Legionnaires of Washington County, traveled to Charlottesville for the state convention. Their mission was to elevate a leader in their local post, Fred Parks, to state commander. The group included Roby Thompson. Attorneys Fred Parks and Roby Thompson were longtime friends and colleagues of the Clark family. They would ultimately team up to prosecute their friend Hal's wife when she went to trial.

Hal Jr., a month from turning seventeen, graduated from William King High School on May 27, 1940, with graduation exercises held at the Sinking Spring Presbyterian Church. His sister Dorothy was twelve years old. Nancy was ten, and Frances was three.

That summer had Little Hal ready to drop the "Little" designation. He had grown tall and willowy, strong and handsome. "OK, here's what I know about Uncle Hal," Gay Leonard stated. "I think Uncle Hal dated every nurse in the nurses' dormitory at the hospital. I'm serious. I don't think he had a girlfriend. He let everybody be in love with him."

Dorothy idolized her older brother and wanted to shoot guns, hunt grouse and work on automobiles just like him. That summer, she hung around the Ropp and Clark Service Station, learning about engines, tires and oil changes. Nancy followed Kathleen DeBose around the kitchen, interested in the techniques of preparing a meal. Frances toddled after them.

For the winters, the family traveled to New Smyrna, Florida. "That started with my grandfather [Hal] because that's where the train went from New York to Florida," Gay Leonard described. "Florida was a horse connection with its stables and racetracks."

In September 1941, Little Hal left for Virginia Polytechnic Institute and State University (VPI). But he rushed home in October to help his mother.

Hal Clark Jr. at sixteen years old. *William King High School's* The Scroll *yearbook, 1939.*

Thursday, October 23, 1941
Bristol News Bulletin
HAL CLARK
ABINGDON, Va., Oct. 23—Hal Clark, 47, prominent Abingdon business man and member of the town council for several terms died suddenly at his home at 4 o'clock Wednesday morning.

His death occurred a few minutes after he suffered a heart attack.

Surviving are his wife and four children, Hal Clark, Jr., Dorothy Ellen, Nancy B., and Frances Evelyn Clark. Five brothers and sisters also survive.

NINETEEN YEARS AFTER THEIR marriage, Helen Talbert Clark was a widow at the age of forty with four children. She'd spent half her life as Hal Clark's wife.

The town leaders, citizens, Hal's siblings, neighbors, business associates and the Talberts couldn't console Helen and the children. No amount of sympathy, comfort, support or solace would soothe the debilitating grief Helen endured. The children realized they would need to tend to the daily needs of the family, since their mother had succumbed, physically and mentally, to her anguish.

Wind whipped crimson and orange leaves along Valley Street. They settled. Helen watched a crow hop down and peck at the leaves until a Chrysler sedan drove east and scattered the crow to flight and the leaves to the automobile's wake. The chilly wind stirred gold maple leaves. They settled. The crow didn't return. Another car, an Oldsmobile Victoria, she thought, sped down the street.

The rocking chair by the parlor's fireplace held Helen's small, frail body. A quilt was tucked around her. Nancy placed a cup of coffee on the table next to her. Did she thank her daughter? She couldn't think. Hal. Where's Hal?

Little Hal and Dorothy—gone to the filling station?

A tiny fairy girl, or maybe Frances, darted around her and up the stairs.

A man with a familiar voice pulled up a chair in front of her. It was C.M., her brother who had helped at the service station. Little Hal? Her head jerked toward C.M. with the question in her eyes. He patted her hand. Had she asked him if Little Hal was OK?

He talked about something. He didn't say "Little Hal." She would have realized that, she convinced herself. He continued speaking to her, close and confidential. Her mother. She wanted her mother. Her mother would make the pain go away—the ache, the loneliness, the despair.

I can't go on. Why, with Hal gone? What did I do that he was taken from me? I will not be left alone. Anger stirred in her. She gripped the quilt on her lap and twisted it into a tight knot. C.M. patted her clenched hands, as if he knew the suffering.

Nancy stood at the dining room doorway, worry lines creasing her young face. C.M. motioned for her to go back to the kitchen.

"Sister, you relax your hands. I'll take care of you," he said.

The reassurance did little to relieve her rage. She didn't want her brother to stay away from his wife and little girls because she had lost her husband. She should have been able to keep Hal alive. What did she do? What did she not do?

The parlor felt like it smothered her. The quilt was on the floor, and perspiration beaded her brow. "Open the door. Let some air in this place." The sound of her voice surprised her—raspy and defeated. She would not be defeated. Hal Clark had shown her how to be powerful and in charge. His smell, the lilac and citrus of Clubman's aftershave, lingered in their bedroom, yet it faded with each day. What if—what if his memory faded in her and the children? Blurred, her eyes couldn't focus on C.M. Gasping for air, she jerked back in the chair, rocking it to slam again the wall.

Nancy ran in and wrapped her arms around her mother. "Do you need Little Hal?" she asked.

"Yes. Yes. Please bring him to me. I need my son." Helen felt the tears burning down her cheek.

C.M. volunteered to go to the service station to retrieve Little Hal and asked Nancy to stay with her mother. Helen knew C.M. was more comfortable at the station than with her. She burdened all those around her. If only I had died instead of Hal. A tremor shuddered her left hand. Calm settled. Is this how death starts? Is this what Hal felt, his body moving without his mind telling it to? God, let it happen to me. I want to go to Hal.

Nancy kissed the top of Helen's head and then said, "I love you."

Her daughter had pulled her back into her body, and she started crying.

Little Hal returned to the university to catch up on his work before his quarterly exams and the Christmas break.

Dorothy and Nancy returned to school. Frances, then only four years old, helped Kathleen DeBose around the house and sat at her mother's chair and played with her dolls while listening to the radio serials. Frances liked to listen to *Fibber McGee and Molly* and *Blondie* on the radio. The comedies rarely made Helen smile, but at times, she would forget—just for a moment—her loss and fall into the radio tomfoolery accented by Frances's giggles. A smile would flicker on her face until she remembered Hal would not be home for supper.

By Sunday, December 7, 1941, Helen had not entered the Presbyterian church since Hal's service. How could she worship a God that had taken Hal from her? In her rocking chair by the parlor fireplace, she stared out the tall window to the west. The newspaper said that President Roosevelt had sent a personal message to Japanese emperor Hirohito on his troop buildup in French Indochina. She turned the page to the list of marriage licenses issued in Abingdon during the previous two weeks. She didn't recognize any of the young couples. On another page, H.P. King's in Bristol advertised a Christmas sale on brocade evening bags and black crepe jackets. Without the Christmas sequins, she could wear the jacket while in mourning.

She looked up from the newspaper. Where were the girls? The sky was clear out the window. Maybe they were playing in the sunny yard, but she could see people bundled up against the cold and rushing along the sidewalk. Was she home by herself? She could not be alone. They knew not to leave her. She listened. The radio was on, and Nancy sat in front of it, flipping through a magazine. How had she not seen Nancy? The side door to the porch slammed. Dorothy and Frances came in with a paper sack, probably candy from the drugstore.

A news report from New York came on. How I loved to visit New York, Helen thought. The announcer was difficult to understand with the crackling sounds interrupting his message. She returned her attention to the newspaper. Dorothy rushed to the radio and turned up the volume. An attack on a naval base in Hawaii, the voice said.

That Christmas, all Hal Jr. could talk about was the war with Japan. The seniors in the corps of cadets at VPI graduated early to join the fight, and the juniors were sped through their leadership training. Sophomores and freshmen were urged toward joining the service to defend the country.

FANNIE TALBERT

The winter of 1942 was difficult for Helen's mother, Fannie. At the age of seventy-nine, her health declined rapidly. Hal's death, just over four months earlier, shadowed Helen as she tried to attend to her mother. Helen's brothers James and John lived in other states. William and C.M. lived in Abingdon and spent time with their father, consoling him of the inevitable death of Fannie. Effie spent day after day with her mother, but Helen couldn't face her mother's deteriorating health. On the morning of March 10, 1942, Frances Elizabeth Davis Talbert died at her home. She was buried in Sinking Spring Cemetery next to her sons Robert and Frank.

CHARLEY TALBERT

Within three months, Charley couldn't go on without Fannie. On June 21, 1942, Charles Matthew Talbert Sr. died of a "lingering illness."

In the span of six months, Helen had lost the three most important adults in her life: her husband, her mother and her father.

LITTLE HAL

On June 29, Hal Jr. turned nineteen years old. The next day, he walked up Courthouse Hill in Abingdon to the old First National Bank building that housed the local draft board and signed his draft card. All the cadets at VPI were signing up for the draft. The school swarmed with tales of war and heroism.

In less than six months, he received the call. He left for Norfolk and was sworn into the navy on December 15, 1942. In September 1943, Hal Jr. shipped out to the South Pacific and Guadalcanal. He participated in the invasion of Bougainville Island in the Solomon Islands on November 1, 1943. For the next two weeks, he helped take territory from the Japanese.

On Saturday, November 20, a Japanese air raid rained down on the Americans at Bougainville. Hal Clark Jr. was wounded. Before he could be transported to the nearest hospital, he died on November 21.

"The day this town got the news that Little Hal had been killed, everybody in Abingdon cried," Gay recounted a longtime resident telling her. "Uncle Hal knew everybody, and they knew him." Hal Jr. had the

Navy photograph of Hal
Clark Jr. *Eva Leonard.*

pedigree, personality and poise to be one of the next generation of leaders of Abingdon.

Dorothy couldn't tolerate her mother's constant crying and fits of rage. Drapes were drawn on all the windows, and the house felt like a tomb. She and her sisters were mourning their brother as much—or more than—their mother, but God forbid anyone besides Helen Clark have a reaction to Little Hal's death. She could fall apart and neglect the house, her children, the filling station. Who did she think would keep the family going? Dad, Grandmother and Granddaddy Talbert—and now Little Hal—all gone in two years' time.

At fifteen years old, Dorothy took control. Nancy, fourteen, helped Kathleen DeBose in the kitchen, and Frances, six, cleaned the house. Dorothy continued to help at the filling station to keep it running with Mr. Ropp and her uncle C.M.

Constant reminders of Hal and Little Hal filled the home. "The house and everything in it was a shrine. Maybe so she could remember," Gay added. "Big Hal's chair was still at the fireplace in the living room. Little Hal's bookcase, his desk and his chair where he did his homework sat in the downstairs hall where he left them." Snowshoes, skis and tennis rackets that Hal and Little Hal used continued to hang on the walls above the side porch doorways.

If the girls had the time to worry about their mother, they would have noticed the deep depression she had developed with the magnitude of her losses in a short amount of time. But the girls ran the household, and Dorothy worked at the filling station. The family's money dwindled. No longer able to pay Kathleen or send the laundry out for cleaning, the girls took on those responsibilities themselves.

Helen sat in her rocking chair and cried.

KITTY SMYTH

With little money coming into the home, Helen and the girls decided to open the house to boarders. The boardinghouse concept had been an acceptable practice for many years, especially for widows with a large home. Jane Douglas Summers Brown, their neighbor at the time, said, "To enhance her income, she took as a boarder a young horse trainer associated in some manner with the Kentucky Derby racetrack." Hal's friends and acquaintances still came to Abingdon for hunting and equestrian events. The Hal Clark home was a familiar place for them, and to the credit of the visitors, they helped the family with their finances. Although the sight of Hal's friends and their condolences to Helen must have reopened emotional wounds for her.

As the fall came around again, a young woman appeared at the Clarks' door. Kitty Smyth introduced herself as an old girlfriend of Hal Jr. and a student at Virginia Intermont College in Bristol. She asked about renting a room.

"Uncle Hal knew everybody. If Kitty had lived in Abingdon, he would have known her," Gay said. "But mother [Dorothy] didn't know her. Aunt Nancy didn't know her. Grandmother [Helen] didn't know her. Nobody had ever heard of her. She showed up and said she was a friend of Hal's, and she needed a place to live. If she knew Little Hal, Grandmother wouldn't send her away."

3

JAMES "JIMMY" EMMETT NEWTON JR.

James "Jimmy" Emmett Newton Jr. was born to James Emmett Newton and Edythe Frances Cowherd Newton on June 11, 1923. His parents were married in June 1908. Emmett, age twenty-four, worked in the insurance industry as an agent. Edythe, age twenty-three, was employed as a stenographer in the Kentucky Viavi Company.

Edythe's employer, the Viavi Company, with locations spread around the globe, peddled their "Viavi Hygiene System" that took vague science of the day and mixed it with common sense to create an industry of cure-alls for women. Using the door-to-door sales methods of the early twentieth century, the Viavi Company recruited an army of middle-aged women to sell home cures that included such practical components like activity and rest, sunshine and fresh air and the importance of a regular routine in a person's day. The Viavi Hygiene System implied that the cause of illness—whether physical, mental or social—was caused by the weakness of mothers.

In the book *Viavi Hygiene*, brothers Hartland and Herbert Law, the authors and entrepreneurs of the Viavi Hygiene System, explained that clean living produced healthy progeny. Medical conditions would occur, and the Viavi Hygiene System had the solution. For the nervous system, mental health, internal organ vitality, wound care, menstruation, pregnancy, a "change of life" and even conditions such as tumors and cancer, the Viavi System suggested self-massage with Viavi cerate; a Viavi douche to be used in the vagina, rectum, nose or ear (depending on the disease being treated); Viavi liquid to drink for kidneys and bladder issues; or the Viavi laxative or enema for any manner of complaints.

Edythe worked her way up in the Louisville office to go from a stenographer to an office manager. Industrious and efficient, Edythe would have been a believer and practitioner of the Viavi System. She made a healthy and disciplined home for Emmett.

Emmett's home life was chaotic when his mother-in-law, Mattie; sister-in-law, Mae; and teenage brother-in-law, Gilbert, moved in with them. Edythe took on the responsibility for her mother, siblings and husband for the next several years.

The Newtons celebrated when Edythe announced her pregnancy. Mabel Lucille Newton was born on her father's thirty-third birthday, January 30, 1917. Edythe was thirty-one. Gilbert and Mae had moved out by then. Edythe found that having her mother live with them was helpful with the baby in their new house in Louisville's Third Ward.

Edythe; her little daughter, Mabel; and her mother, Mattie, filled the house with feminine empowerment. The concept of Edythe's employer and its Viavi System of clean living began to fade in the wake of World War I and the Spanish flu pandemic. Women were more than vessels for the next generation.

The war had helped expand the United States' industrial economy. The cities grew suburbs that sprawled like mushrooms across the countryside. The Newtons' new home was in Anchorage, Kentucky, on the eastern outskirts of Louisville.

Mabel was six years old when her baby brother arrived in June 1923. The baby was named after his thirty-nine-year-old father. James Emmett Newton Jr. was called Jimmy. The family now consisted of Emmett and Edythe, their daughter and son and grandmother Mattie.

Not all aspects of the Viavi regimen had faded from Edythe's life. Here was an opportunity to shape the development of a boy who would become a successful and influential man. After having a son at the age of thirty-eight, Edythe had the confidence and gumption to shape the boy into a great man.

At the age of four and a half, Jimmy began a rigorous study of the violin. "Jimmy had a great love for music," Edythe explained to Evelyn Hicks, a *Bristol Herald Courier* reporter, years later. "He took piano lessons but had a natural gift and could play with or without music. He also had a good voice and loved to sing. While he was going to school, he had a program over the radio station back home."

Emmett, a man of few words, added to his wife's description of their son: "Jimmy liked sports but hated trouble. Whenever an argument arose on the playing field, he always acted in the role of a peacemaker. He never would fight with anyone."

An automobile wreck injured young Jimmy at the age of ten, according to his father. The account from Emmett mentions this accident only in passing, describing that Jimmy was injured "about the head and face." Emmett suggested that Jimmy may have had some lingering pain from this car accident. There is no reference to who had driven the car, where the wreck occurred or if other people had been hurt. Jimmy's photographs from his teen and military years show no physical signs of injury.

Jimmy attended Anchorage and Louisville Male High Schools. He participated in music programs and sports. He was active in the Boy Scouts. An attractive young man, Jimmy seemed to be popular with his classmates. The other boys flocked to him and his charisma and energy. The young girls enjoyed his singing and polite attention.

Kentucky Boy Champ Arrives for Final Meet

At the beginning of his junior year at Anchorage High School, Jimmy was named the Kentucky winner of the Ford Good Drivers League's national driving contest. Jimmy's interest in automobiles and safety may have stemmed from the accident he was in at the age of ten. As the Kentucky winner, Jimmy traveled to the New York World's Fair in August 1940.

Edythe suggested to Emmett that she travel with Jimmy to New York. She paced in front of Emmett's chair. The *Louisville Courier-Journal* obscured her husband's face and hid his openness to her trip with their son.

Emmett exhaled like a locomotive releasing its steam. He lowered the newspaper just enough for her to see him. "Edy, let the boy have an adventure," Emmett said. He glanced back down to the business section of the paper. Emmett had his insurance agency on his mind, and his wife needed to give Jimmy some room to grow. She'd watched him like a mother hen from the time he was born. Emmett looked up from his newspaper again and added, "He'll be there with forty-seven other boys, all excellent students, all state winners. He's seventeen. He's a good kid. Let him have some fun. Don't over-mother the boy."

HERE'S J. E. Newton, Jr., of Anchorage, Kentucky's state champion boy automobile driver. He's shown as he arrived at the Ford Motor pavilion at the New York World's Fair, ready to compete in the finals to determine the national boy driving champion. Newton's expenses, and those of an adult sponsor chosen by himself, were paid by the Ford Good Drivers League. At the first annual Champions' Banquet at the Ford pavilion on Aug. 29, Edsel Ford, president of the League, was scheduled to award the prizes—48 university scholarships with an aggregate value of $30,000. The object of the League is to promote safety on the highways by teaching every boy in America to drive expertly. It has a membership of scores of thousands of boys in all parts of the country.

Jimmy Newton, Kentucky's Ford Good Driver champion. *From the* Advocate Messenger *(Louisville, KY).*

The newspaper reported on the pending Conscription Act, a peacetime draft registration for young men and a signal that the war in Europe could reach over to the States. Emmett had not been called into World War I, but Jimmy could be drafted in a few years if the conflicts in Europe escalated.

"Be that as it may," Edythe began, "the Ford people said a guardian must accompany each boy. That would be me or you."

Emmett looked out the window by his chair and caught sight of Jimmy walking along the sidewalk, returning from choir practice. He seemed so carefree. These are the days, Emmett thought, that a boy has the time to develop into the man that makes his family proud. Those sons of bitches in Europe need to leave our boy out of their quarrel and let him grow into a man.

He didn't want Jimmy to feel like a child on this trip by having his mother or father with him. "Gil. Gil could go as Jimmy's guardian. He's the one who taught Jimmy how to drive."

"My brother Gil?" Edythe asked. Then she shook her head. She crossed the room and settled on the arm of Emmett's chair. "Why not you? But, really, Gil and Jimmy together in New York? I'd rather go myself."

He wanted to snap at her, but he calmed himself, knowing that she considered Jimmy her baby. She paid little attention to Mabel. Their daughter planned to marry Lem, a man over ten years older than her. And dollars to doughnuts, Lem would move in with them.

The front door opened, and Jimmy bounded in. "Jim, do you think your uncle Gil would make an appropriate guardian for your Ford competition in New York? Your mother and I think it's time for you to get out from under our wings."

"Yes, sir!" Jimmy stood straight and saluted his father. "Call me the eager beaver. Oh, thank you." He rushed over and hugged Edythe, still sitting on the arm of Emmett's chair. He shook his father's hand. "Uncle Gil would be swell to travel with. You can count on me to do Kentucky good at the competition."

Edythe stood, straightened her dress and crossed her arms. "I'd feel better if Mabel or I accompanied him," she said to Emmett.

Jimmy's eyes shifted from his mother to his father with an imploring knit of his eyebrows.

"He needs a man with him," Emmett said. "I can't take a week off from work. Gil would be happy to go. I will have my secretary make the train reservations and confirm the hotel with Ford. Edy, you get Gil on board. Tell him it's 'all expenses paid.' That will set it with him."

The 1939–40 New York World's Fair celebrated "The World of Tomorrow" with the latest technological innovations and a vision for the future. The exposition was housed in the Borough of Queens at Flushing Meadows. In the recent aftermath of World War I, the Spanish flu pandemic and the Depression, visitors couldn't help but be inspired by the exposition's buildings and programs.

The last week of August 1940, Jimmy traveled by train to Grand Central Terminal and checked in at the Commodore Hotel at 109 East Forty-Second Street. A guardian accompanied each state champion to the Ford Good Drivers League final competition, and assuming Emmett's business obligations and Edythe's attention on Mabel's wedding, Gilbert seemed to be a logical choice for Jimmy's chaperone.

In the National Archives, a newsreel highlights the 1940 Ford Good Drivers League final competition at the World's Fair. All the boys wore matching navy blue and white jackets, and each was awarded a gold, engraved wristwatch. Mayor Fiorello La Guardia welcomed the boys to New York City at the opening luncheon.

During the competition, each contestant completed a series of tests, including eye tests, physical reaction tests and several driving skills tests. While the results were tabulated, the forty-eight boys and their guardians were treated to tours around the city, including a boat sightseeing excursion around Manhattan. In the newsreel, Jimmy is clearly seen enjoying the band on the deck of the boat. He's singing, a bespectacled friend's arm draped casually over his shoulder, as the band plays.

The $5,000 scholarship grand prize winner was the boy from Indiana, with the Arizona contestant coming in second with a $2,000 scholarship. Jimmy, along with the other state winners, received a $100 scholarship, and he had his first taste of adventure.

At the Commodore Hotel, Gil decided to let Jimmy explore with some of the other boys. He's only here for a couple more days, Gill thought, let him discover the town with his friends. Gil headed to the hotel's bar.

Jimmy had become close with a young man from a southern state who looked like Li'l Abner from the comic strips—except Li'l Abner didn't wear wire-rimmed glasses like Luke did. Luke had a friendly personality and loved music, just like Jimmy. Luke's boldness took some getting used to for Jimmy, but as Luke said, "We're only in New York for week—time to make some memories."

Luke and Jimmy ditched their blue Good Driver jackets and gold wristwatches in their rooms. Thursday, August 29, 1940, in midtown Manhattan was unusually mild, with a high temperature of 72 degrees, a perfect day for the boys to investigate the Manhattan neighborhoods. They walked west along Forty-Second Street to Times Square.

Top: Jimmy Newton (*far right*) on a sightseeing excursion with the 1940 Ford Good Drivers League at the World's Fair. *National Archives at College Park, Motion Pictures; Ford Motor Company Collection.*

Bottom: A 1940 Ford Good Drivers League newsreel of Jimmy Newton (*second from left*) on a sightseeing boat enjoying the band. *National Archives at College Park, Motion Pictures; Ford Motor Company Collection.*

Bright, flashy movie theater marquees and billboards as large as train cars lined the square. It was the hubbub of the city's culture. Luke pointed to a movie house marquee displaying *My Favorite Wife*, starring Cary Grant, Irene Dunne and Randolph Scott. "That Cary Grant is my favorite," Luke said. "I already saw that picture. He's got a new one showing next month." Luke threw his arm over Jimmy's shoulder. "You kind of look like his buddy Randolph Scott."

"Did you see *Coast Guard*, where Randolph Scott played Speed Bradshaw? Movies make war seem exciting," Jimmy said. His enthusiasm dwindled with the thought of war. He pulled away from Luke and sat on a step near the theater. "Do you think we'll end up fighting overseas?"

Luke sat next to him. "I hope not. I'm no coward, but I don't think I could kill a person, even to defend my country or myself." He adjusted his glasses and then leaned over and bumped his shoulder against Jimmy's. "If we're called, let's enlist together."

Jimmy smiled. "Army? Navy? Coast guard, like Randolph Scott?"

"Naw," Luke said as he grinned back at him. "Marines. They're the best." Luke leaned against Jimmy for a few seconds then sat back and nudged him. "Want a beer, marine?"

"Honest? I mean—can we get one?" Jimmy asked.

"One? I'll buy you a couple, and then you can buy me a couple. You got moxie. I can tell by that gleam in your baby blues. We won't tell anyone. Just you and me—it's between us. We'll get a buzz, play around some. Let's have some fun."

Later that evening, Gil began to worry, since he hadn't seen Jimmy come back through the lobby. But then, Gil had gone out with some of the fathers to a burlesque show. He smoked cigars and had a drink at the hotel bar, watching the lobby for any sighting of his nephew. He decided to go back to the room. When he opened the door, he heard snickering and shuffling. "You boys quiet down," Gil scolded them. "You'll get the hotel manager up here, and we'll all get kicked out. Just 'cause you're from Kentucky, Jimmy, you don't have to act like it." He looked to Luke rolling on the floor in a fit of giggles. "You had anything to eat?"

"Eat?" He heaved a little. Gil grabbed the boy and lifted him off the floor, and then he carried him to the bathroom. "Jimmy, get your pants on. We're going to the coffee shop to sober you two up."

The boys sat with Gil in the lobby's coffee shop, sipping black coffee and sneaking looks at each other. Gil watched them and smiled. "If Edy finds out about this, she'll have your hide and mine," he told Jimmy.

Back home, Edythe didn't discover Jimmy and Gil's antics. Jimmy and Luke continued their friendship through letters mailed on a regular basis. Eventually, the letters weren't sent or received regularly, as life brought in other priorities for both young men.

⚬⚬⚬

ON DECEMBER 7, 1941, the United States reeled in shock from the Japanese attack on the naval base at Pearl Harbor. Many young men discussed their obligations to their country around the dinner tables, and in the days leading up to Christmas, Jimmy decided that he should stand with his country. His mother, father, sister and her husband, Lem, couldn't talk him out of joining the fight. He was a healthy young man. President Roosevelt had called to action the men of the United States.

The January 1942 U.S. Marine muster rolls lists James E. Newton Jr. in the Third Recruit Battalion at Parris Island, South Carolina. By July 1942, Private First Class Newton was mustered in New River, North Carolina. While at New River, Jimmy befriended Private Leslie Clarke Beetlestone.

Clarke Beetlestone was the son of Leslie Thomas Kirby Beetlestone and Erna Luise Loewe Beetlestone. Jimmy and Clarke had parents in their mid- to late fifties and sisters several years older than them. The Beetlestones lived in the Borough of Bogota, New Jersey. Bogota was less than ten miles from Manhattan.

GUADALCANAL OFFENSIVE

After the Doolittle Raid on Tokyo in April 1942—as a payback for Pearl Harbor—the United States was on the defensive against Japanese expansion in the Pacific. The U.S. Navy's victory at the Battle of Midway in June proved that.

The Japanese had established a base in Rabaul on the Island of New Britain in Papua New Guinea. From this strategic base, the Japanese could interrupt supply and communication routes between the United States and Australia.

In July, an intelligence agent reported that the Japanese were unloading construction equipment on the north coast of the island of Guadalcanal, part of the Solomon Islands. With an airfield on Guadalcanal, the Japanese would further their defensive line and create a staging area for possible attacks on Australia and its neighboring countries.

Admiral Ernest King wanted to take Guadalcanal before the Japanese airfield was operational. He set the invasion date for August, a logistical Hail Mary, that gave the United States a month to get troops, ships, aircraft and strategies in place.

Jimmy and Clarke had trained at New River in the marine's transport procedures. October's muster role finds them both in Guadalcanal. The environment of Guadalcanal is one of the harshest in the South Pacific. Near the equator, the island's hot and rainy climate creates a thick, wet blanket of a jungle. The southern mountains rise to over 7,800 feet.

On August 7, 1942, the marines hit Guadalcanal's northern shore, to the surprise of the few Japanese construction workers at the airstrip site. The construction crews ran for the jungle. The marines took Guadalcanal. Their next step was to keep it.

Serving on Guadalcanal in those first months, from August to October 1942, caused the men to reestablish their concept of living. Tropical disease and malnutrition were as deadly as enemy fire. The marines' supplies dwindled. After the capture of the airstrip site, they found a cache of rice left by the Japanese workers. This rice became their source of food until ships were able return with more supplies. Veterans, years later, talked of

> the lack of food and the constant daily rations of the maggot- and worm-infested rice issued to them by the 1st Marine Division's cooks, who ate the same unappetizing two-tablespoon meal day after day. Combined with the hot, humid weather, the stress of combat, and the inadequate diet, the men ashore lost weight at an acute rate. The marines ashore, children of the Great Depression, were already thin and soon became downright skinny. It was not uncommon for men on Guadalcanal to lose as much as 40 pounds due to malnutrition and tropical diseases.

Even with malnourishment and the threat of malaria from swarms of mosquitoes, the marines' completion of the airstrip took priority, and the first marine fighter planes landed by the end of August. The ship that carried Jimmy's battalion arrived with supplies, and the marines helped relieve the men who had held the island for the previous several weeks.

A navy corpsman gives a drink to a wounded marine in Guam. *Official U.S. Navy photograph, Library of Congress; Guam, July 1944; https://www.loc.gov/item/94502155/.*

A casualty from the front line is transferred through the jungle and down the river to a hospital. *Library of Congress; Guadalcanal, Solomon Islands; https://www.loc.gov/item/2017872091/.*

Jimmy transferred from the ship to an amphibious landing craft loaded with vehicles, equipment and troops. He moved everything and everyone from the transport craft to the beach then assisted with the reinforcements for the marines staying on the island. Some of the marines went back to the ship for a well-deserved break from the sweltering jungle, while Jimmy and his troops took their place for a few days. This was real combat. Jimmy had trained for this, but his actual assignments tended to be more support oriented. He worried about his performance. Could he shoot someone? On the ship, his enemy engagements had been distant, impersonal aircraft, unseen submarines or anonymous cruisers. He never saw the face of the enemy. The guys in the battalion talked of Japanese fighters running at them with their guns firing. Bullets ricocheted from rocks, tree trunks and even helmets on dead bodies. The situation was kill or be killed. The worst possible outcome was to be captured by the enemy.

Attacks on the U.S. troops came at night. The Japanese would sneak into the harbor in the dark, their destroyers used as troop carriers. They would drop off thousands of their soldiers before hightailing it back toward the safety of Rabaul and out of range of the U.S. aircraft.

On his third rotation from the transport crafts to relieving the marines holding Henderson Field, Jimmy's mood heartened when his friend Clarke "Beet" Beetlestone plopped down beside him on his evening watch.

"Jim, fancy running into you here," Clarke said as he positioned his gun toward the fringe of the jungle thicket. "Seems we're on watch together." Clarke favored his mother's German ancestry more than his father's English side. He was tall and naturally fair, but his months with the marines in South Carolina and North Carolina and then in the Pacific had tanned his skin to a light chestnut with a perpetual red tinge.

"Glad to see a friendly face, Beet," Jimmy said. "The Japs are building up troops on the other side of the island. That tangle of trees and vines have kept the Japs back. At night, I can hear those bastards hacking away at that undergrowth. They could chop through at any time." He focused back on the tree line. "You heard from anyone back home?"

Beet shook his head. "No. They say mail isn't making it through. I know they're thinking about us."

"Maybe your family is, but sometimes, I wonder about mine." Jimmy exhaled, long and plaintive. "This island could be it for me."

"Come on, man," Beet said. "You got all of us marines. We're your family, now. I will take care of you, and you take care of me—brothers."

The idea of having a brother improved Jimmy's outlook. Over the months they had known each other, Jimmy felt like he'd confided more to Beet than he had to anyone else in his entire life. He glanced over at Beet, who was staring at the swaying grasses that led to the jungle. "Beet, I got to admit that I'm a little scared." Sweat rolled down Jimmy's face, and he wiped it away.

Beet turned his head to Jimmy, biting his bottom lip in a half grimace. He raised one eyebrow. "Jim, me, too. Me, too, brother. The only solace I have is that you're here with me."

They talked and kept watch through the sunset; other marines relieved them of their post for a few hours. The almost constant rainfall tried to rust their guns, so when they were away from the front line, the men cleaned and oiled their rifles and heavy artillery. Just as the Allied troops were delivering supplies, weapons and men to the north shore, Jimmy knew the Japanese were doing the same on the other side of the island.

Another watch came for Jimmy and Beet on the ridge by the jungle. This one started at 3:00 a.m. The humidity pressed down on their skin. The men had long ago shed their regulation uniforms and wore as little as possible—just enough to keep the insects and sun's rays off them. Since the shift occurred during the night, their main concern was the biting bugs. Jimmy and Beet wore their helmets and unbuttoned their shirts, since the slight breeze on their skin was worth the bites from the insects. Their khakis and boots protected them while they were hunched on the ground. They talked about nothing in particular but listened intently, as if each would quiz the other.

"You! American!" Shouts came from the jungle. "See you! Find us! Ha!"

Beet and Jimmy grabbed their guns tight and strained to see in the dark. "What the hell is that?" Beet asked.

"Damn. Some of the guys say the Japs get close and yell at us. Their English ain't shit, but they're enthusiastic in their taunts."

One of the marines up the line from them yelled back. "Hey, Jap! Suck my big American willy!"

Pop. Crack. Pew. Ping. Whracck. Bullets pelted around them.

"That asshole Wilson took their bait," Jimmy said as he fired back toward the flashes from the Japanese shooting.

"Oh, hell, this is fun," Beet said, and then he pushed the stripper clip into the magazine of his rifle and fired off round after round.

The firefight lit up the dark night. Jimmy heard more marines coming to the line, alerted by the clamor of the guns. A flash in the dark appeared closer than the tree line—then another and another. The Japanese had cleared the jungle and ran toward the ridge, firing as they advanced.

Marine reinforcements rammed in with their night watch. They fired at the flashes spraying from the Japanese guns. With the barrage of crossfire, the night ignited into a strobe of orange-yellow streaks. Jimmy's eyes blurred from the muzzle flashes in the dark. He couldn't aim but kept firing with lowered eyelids to protect his pupils from the glare.

"Hold the line!" their platoon lieutenant roared. Jimmy heard the rattle of the howitzers lining up and their chest-thumping *booms*. The reverberation of the firing knocked his breath out of him. The jungle seemed to explode with screams and more rifle fire. The Japanese could not have brought heavy artillery through the jungle. They had nothing but rifles, knives and no regard for life—theirs or the Americans'.

Jimmy reached over to make sure Beet was still next to him. With the bombardment of noise and blinding muzzle flashes, Jimmy's only reassurance was grabbing Beet's belt. "Don't go over the line," he yelled into Beet's ear. "Get yourself killed by our own guns. Stay put."

The M240G units joined the fight. The machine guns incorporated a guard to minimize the muzzle flash and not give away their locations, but the fight had already begun, and the marines' line was well established. The guns' visual stealth wasn't of much use at this point, but they compensated with rapid firing.

The rifles the Japanese had packed through the jungle couldn't compare to the raw power of the Americans' arsenal. The Americans beat them back into the thicket. The attacks subsided but then started again. Jimmy, Beet and some of the overnight watch rolled off the line as more marines came in with better weapons.

The constant artillery bombardment made rest difficult. The oppressive humidity had Jimmy and Clarke lying on bare sheets on their cots, hoping for a breeze to come through the tent. Any chance of sleep eluded them. Images of the past hours crept into Jimmy's mind—visions of black night slashed with orange flashes; cries of angry attacks, wretched pain and battering gunfire; odors of pungent gun powder, sour sweat and rusty iron blood.

"We made it, Jim," Beet whispered from the next cot.

A tear slipped down the side of Jimmy's face and puddled in his ear. He hoped the tent was dark enough that Beet wouldn't see. "God help us." He wiped his eyes and then rolled to his side to try to make out Beet in the night. "I shot several men. I saw them in flashes. They were close, running toward us. Like they had a suicide wish. I know we were told in boot camp that the Japs considered their troops expendable, but damn, Beet, how can a man get to that point of throwing his body in front of machine guns, as if using up the opponent's ammunition is worth his life? I can't understand—" his words choked in his throat. Then a sob escaped.

Beet slid off his cot and kneeled next to Jimmy's face, close enough to see each other. "Listen to me. We did what we had to do to save our own lives and the lives of our squad. The marines tried to prepare us. But, who?" His voice softened. "Who could toughen a person enough for that?"

"How do we go back home after this?" Jimmy asked. "I don't think I could walk down the street and look someone in the eye without seeing sliced-open bodies and blood."

The other marines seemed to have found sleep, confirmed by the sounds of regular breathing and snores. With the dark of the tent, no one could see more than a few inches away from their face, but Beet was within that range with Jimmy. "I try to separate myself—my real self—from this warrior self," Beet said. "When I fired my rifle, I could almost see the real me hovering above my body. I felt I watched a movie. Not until we were called back here did my human soul slip back into my body." He reached around and hugged Jimmy. "Clear your mind. Get some rest, buddy." With that, he climbed back into his cot.

BRINGING WOUNDED
DOWN MATANIKAU RIVER

Artist Howard Brodie's drawing of marines transporting the wounded during Jimmy Newton's deployment to Guadalcanal, Solomon Islands. *Library of Congress, https://www.loc. gov/item/2004661748/.*

The sunrise lightened the tent's interior. The men stirred. Silence filled the dawn air. At breakfast in the mess hall, the platoon lieutenant reported the casualties from the night's combat. On September 13, 1942, with air and sea support, the 830 marines on Guadalcanal resisted the continual attacks of as many as 3,000 Japanese troops. With the dawn, the Japanese retreated, leaving over 800 dead. The Americans lost 59.

The next day, Beet found Jimmy on the ship's deck, smoking a cigarette. "Jim, our company just got our orders. I'm heading to Funafuti." He chuckled. "Should be a good time: *Fun-a-futi*. We're defense there. Have you got any word on your company?"

He offered Beet a Lucky Strike from his pack and his Zippo lighter. "We're here—transport equipment and supplies. I think you're going to *Foo-na-foo-tee*, but *Fun-a-futi* could be the Jersey pronunciation."

"OK, wise ass. As if a Kentucky boy is so cultured." Beet laughed and shouldered up to Jimmy at the deck's railing. "When we get discharged, come up to Jersey. There's plenty of opportunity around Manhattan. You said you liked your trip there. I tell you, the city is buzzing. You have my address." Beet looked out to sea and sighed. "If you get stateside before me, let my parents know I'm doing swell. Lie to them," he added with a laugh. "Really, it hasn't been a year yet since Pearl Harbor. Mail can't get through."

"Supplies take priority," Jimmy said.

"I know, but it sure would be good to hear from home."

"OK. If I get home before you, I will go see your parents. If you get back first, you do the same for me."

Beet agreed. He flicked his cigarette over the railing. "Although we'll see each other before the end of this war, I want you to know that having a buddy like you has made this tolerable, if not pleasurable at times."

Jimmy glanced up at the clear blue sky and smiled. Had he ever had a close friend before? He couldn't remember anyone like Clarke Beetlestone. Military service threw men together from all backgrounds, men who probably would never have interacted in civilian life. They worked together, they lived together, they went to battle together, they took care of each other. "Thank you, Clarke."

Clarke grinned at Jimmy for using his given name instead of Beet.

"You are my best buddy," Jimmy confessed. "We'll be assigned together in a few more weeks. In the meantime, I'm going to think up some New York City jobs for us."

The October 1942 muster lists Private Leslie Clarke Beetlestone with Company Y, Defense Force, Fifth Defensive Battalion, stationed at Funafuti on Ellice Island (now Tuvalu).

Private First Class James E. Newton Jr. continued at Guadalcanal until October 18, 1942. A few days earlier, the Japanese increased their assaults on American positions on the island. During a rushed landing operation of supplies, vehicles and weapons, Jimmy became trapped between supply crates and fell from one deck to another. He sustained head injuries and a fractured hip. He was flown to the marine base at Tutuila, Samoa. His injuries were extensive, and the next day, Monday, October 19, the marines transported him to the military hospital in San Diego, California. Jimmy spent four months in that hospital.

Before World War II, post-traumatic stress disorder (PTSD) was referred to as shell shock. As the military learned more about the condition during World War II, it was labeled combat fatigue. At the beginning of the war, military doctors believed combat fatigue affected only those with some underlying mental condition. Maybe their psychological strength wasn't up to par. During screenings, the War Department looked for "weak constitutions" or "mental deficiencies" that could lead a soldier to break down during combat. "However, after the Guadalcanal Campaign, the U.S. military learned that a serviceman's ability to survive the psychological rigors of combat could not be predicted," explained the National World War II Museum's former curator and U.S. Army veteran Larry Decuers. "The point was driven home when, in 1943, one of the nation's elite fighting forces suffered significant psychiatric casualties. More than five hundred marines returning from Guadalcanal were treated for symptoms such as tremors, sensitivity to loud noises and periods of amnesia—the condition was termed 'Guadalcanal Disorder.'"

Jimmy was a "nervous wreck," his father said in court. After Jimmy's return to Kentucky, he was medically discharged from the service.

There is no cure for PTSD. Psychotherapy and medications help with symptoms today, but in 1943, the self-treatment many returning military found included rest, distraction, alcohol and drugs. Drugs used during World War II included Benzedrine (or "bennies"), a stimulant used to combat anxiety, sleep deprivation and fatigue; alcohol for mood adjustment and depression; heroin; morphine tablets; and cocaine. Speed kept the war going. According to American Recovery Centers' writer Brittany Tackett, "The Pentagon issued between 250–500 million Benzedrine tablets to U.S. troops during the war."

FROM FEBRUARY 1943 TO that fall, Jimmy attempted to recover at home with his family. He had been halfway through his senior year of high school when he joined the marines, so as he felt better, he decided to enroll at the Kentucky Military Institute (KMI) to finish his high school education.

KENTUCKY MILITARY INSTITUTE

Before starting the winter session at KMI, Jimmy traveled to Oak Ridge, Tennessee, where he met Kitty Smyth. The Clinton Engineer Works and

Tennessee Eastman Corporation ran employment advertisements in the regional newspapers. The secretive Manhattan Project had three primary sites in the United States: Los Alamos, New Mexico; Hanford, Washington; and Oak Ridge, Tennessee. Oak Ridge, at that time, was ramping up for the plants and laboratories that would produce plutonium. Many area residents were hired to work, but few knew what their objective was. Jimmy traveled down from Kentucky and met Kitty Smyth in Oak Ridge, Tennessee, in December 1943.

He started school in January 1944 at the Kentucky Military Institute. His experience in the marines was a great benefit to him, as it was to the other young men at the military school. The military structure also helped him step from full Pacific combat mode to a hybrid military/civilian existence and then back to full civilian life. After his ten months of recovery at his parents' home, the boarding school was a welcome reprieve from the watchful eyes of his mother, Edythe. He wanted to be around young men his age, as he had been in the marines. Especially attractive was the fact that KMI had a winter campus in Venice, Florida, which meant Jimmy spent the winter months of 1944 on the Gulf Coast, again a step back to normalcy in the mild Florida climate, a point between the oppressive heat of the South Pacific and the bitter cold of a Kentucky winter.

The KMI loaded its students, faculty and staff on a train and headed south for the winter term. The campus in Venice provided the boys with the warmth of their friends and teachers in the Florida sun. The prospect of spending three months almost one thousand miles from home must have been a paradise for these young men, especially Jimmy, who was two years older than the other seniors at the school. During this time, Jimmy corresponded with Kitty Smyth. She explained that he wrote to ask her to go to KMI spring dances in Florida several times, but she did not go.

With or without a girlfriend, Jimmy seemed to savor his time in Florida. The cadets had many opportunities to mix with the local boys. The KMI sports teams competed with the area high schools, prep schools and junior colleges. In the mild weather of the Florida winter, the boys played tennis and golf, along with basketball, baseball, football and wrestling. Although his physical injuries held him back, Jimmy participated when he could. He had regained the weight he lost in Guadalcanal and during his recovery. Jimmy stood six feet tall and weighed 180 pounds.

If he was not able to be a standout athlete because of the war, he had his musical talents. Music helped soothe his nerves, as he lost himself in the compositions, and music boosted his popularity with the other cadets

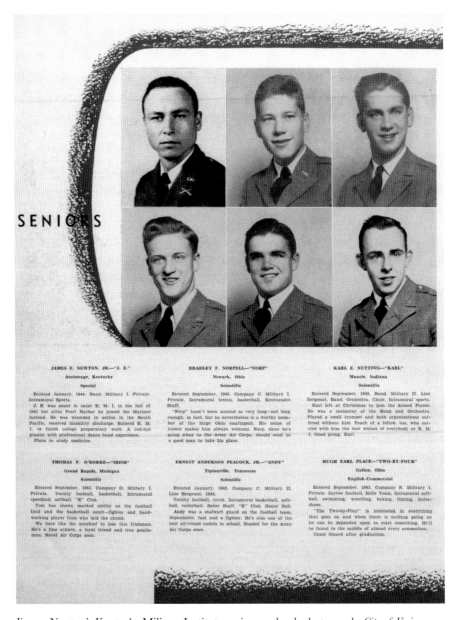

SENIORS

JAMES E. NEWTON, JR.—"J. E."

Anchorage, Kentucky

Special

Entered January, 1944. Band. Military I. Private. Intramural Sports.

J. E. was about to enter K. M. I. in the fall of 1941 but after Pearl Harbor he joined the Marines instead. He was wounded in action in the South Pacific, received disability discharge. Entered K. M. I. to finish college preparatory work. A red-hot pianist with professional dance band experience. Plans to study medicine.

BRADLEY F. NORPELL—"NORP"

Newark, Ohio

Scientific

Entered September, 1943. Company C. Military I. Private. Intramural tennis, basketball. Kentucadet Staff.

"Norp" hasn't been around so very long—not long enough, in fact, but he nevertheless is a worthy member of the large Ohio contingent. His sense of humor makes him always welcome. Norp, since he's going away to the Army Air Corps, should send us a good man to take his place.

KARL E. NUTTING—"KARL"

Muncie, Indiana

Scientific

Entered September, 1942. Band. Military II. Line Sergeant. Band, Orchestra, Choir, Intramural sports.

Karl left at Christmas to join the Armed Forces. He was a mainstay of the Band and Orchestra. Played a swell trumpet and both organizations suffered without him. Peach of a fellow, too, who carried with him the best wishes of everybody at K. M. I. Good going, Karl.

THOMAS F. O'RORKE—"IRISH"

Grand Rapids, Michigan

Scientific

Entered September, 1943. Company D. Military I. Private. Varsity football, basketball, Intramural speedball, softball. "K" Club.

Tom has shown marked ability on the football field and the basketball court—fighter and hardworking player from who laid the chunk.

We hate like the mischief to lose this Irishman. He's a fine athlete, a loyal friend and true gentleman. Naval Air Corps soon.

ERNEST ANDERSON PEACOCK, JR.—"ANDY"

Tiptonville, Tennessee

Scientific

Entered January, 1943. Company C. Military II. Line Sergeant, 1944.

Varsity football, track. Intramural basketball, softball, volleyball. Saber Staff. "K" Club. Honor Roll.

Andy was a stalwart guard on the football team, dependable, fast and a fighter. He's also one of the best all-round cadets in school. Headed for the Army Air Corps soon.

HUGH EARL PLACE—"TWO-BY-FOUR"

Galion, Ohio

English-Commercial

Entered September, 1943. Company B. Military I. Private. Jayvee football, Rifle Team. Intramural softball, swimming, wrestling, boxing, fishing, horseshoes.

"The Two-by-Four" is interested in everything that goes on and when there is nothing going on he can be depended upon to start something. He'll be found in the middle of almost every commotion. Coast Guard after graduation.

Jimmy Newton's Kentucky Military Institute senior yearbook photograph. *City of Venice, Florida Division of Historical Resources.*

and the Florida residents. He sang with the choir at the local Episcopalian church and played the piano in the dormitories and the dining hall and at off-campus gatherings. "A red-hot pianist with professional dance band experience," the KMI yearbook for 1944 said of Jimmy.

The lure of the gulf endeared the cadets to Florida. The boys spent their evenings and weekends—as often as the faculty allowed them—on the beach and in the surf. Jimmy and his friends had time to explore South Florida. He returned to Kentucky to graduate with his high school diploma.

UNIVERSITY OF KENTUCKY

In the fall of 1944, Jimmy enrolled in the University of Kentucky. Kitty Smyth enrolled in Virginia Intermont College in Bristol, Virginia.

Because of his Guadalcanal injuries, Jimmy wasn't able to participate in intramural sports at the University of Kentucky. Instead, he supported the teams by joining the cheerleading squad.

Jimmy's bus trip to a basketball game in New York City in December 1944 had two objectives. Jimmy wanted to visit Clarke Beetlestone's parents in New Jersey. He had written them once he was back in the States, just as Beet had asked. Jimmy had also written to Beet through the marines' channels, but he didn't think his letters would make it through. The Beetlestones had asked Jimmy to visit anytime. Secondly, there was a bus route that would take him through southwestern Virginia, where Kitty Smyth was boarding at the home of a widow and her children.

4

THE INSTIGATOR

GENOA KATHLEEN "KITTY" SMYTH

Genoa Kathleen "Kitty" Smyth was born on February 15, 1925, a Valentine's Day gift to her parents, Gordon Lee Smyth and Myrtle Otelia Johnson Smyth. Her father, Gordon, was twenty-one years old when he married Myrtle, who was just fifteen years old, in 1924. The next year, Kitty was born, and she and her mother seemed to grow up together.

Kitty came from a hardworking and ambitious family. Her great-granduncle was Tobias Smyth, who helped found the College of Emory and Henry in Emory, Virginia.

As the Depression hit the area, Gordon took his young family east. Gordon secured a job at Langley Air Force Base in Hampton, Virginia. Myrtle didn't care for Hampton and the buzz of the military base. Myrtle was twenty-six, and Kitty was ten years old. The girls, Myrtle and Kitty, decided to move back to Southwest Virginia without Gordon. They rented a house in Abingdon. Myrtle secured a job as a bookkeeper with the state's welfare office near Abingdon.

Scarce information is available on Kitty as a teenager to summon a personality based on those early facts, but her later life depicts her ambition coupled with misjudgments. From Kitty's testimony at the Clark trial, she stated she first encountered Jimmy Newton in December 1943. In December 1944, Jimmy stopped in Abingdon to see Kitty on his way to New York. Was she Jimmy's "sweetheart?" Why did he make the trip to Abingdon? She was the only voice for Jimmy at the trial on his reasoning, expectations and state of mind when he came to Abingdon on that snowy evening in 1944.

Her life after the trial illustrated her folly, rashness and lapses in judgment.

In 1950, at the age of twenty-five, Kitty moved to Phoenix, Arizona. She married Richard H. Voorhis, a recently divorced radio executive from the East Coast. Kitty's mother and father moved to Phoenix as well.

Kitty's father, Gordon Smyth, died in Phoenix in 1952. Richard traveled to radio conventions around the country. In early 1954, he accepted a job in Memphis. Memphis did not agree with Kitty—neither did life with Richard. She sued Richard for divorce in November 1955. The *Memphis Press-Scimitar* reported, "They separated Aug. 26 and charges cruel and inhuman treatment." Kitty moved back to Phoenix to live with her widowed mother.

In Arizona in 1957, Kitty Smyth Voorhis worked as a clerk with Hospital Benefit Assurance. Her mother, Myrtle, worked as a stenographer with the State Highway Department. Both women lived together at the La Paloma Apartments at 317 West Portland Street in downtown Phoenix.

William Niles Raisor passed several bogus checks around the Tucson area, and in 1957, he was serving time in the federal penitentiary in Leavenworth, Kansas. By April 1958, William Raisor, also known as W.E. Roberts and William Savage, had been released from Leavenworth and was back in Tucson for his arraignment on two counts of bogus checks, with another hearing on grand theft and a third on passing another bad check.

No record exists to hint at how Kitty met William Raisor after his release from federal prison in 1958. But she did meet him. She liked him, and he liked her. On May 31, 1958, thirty-three-year-old Kitty and forty-one-year-old William Raisor were married in Las Vegas.

When William Raisor went before Superior Court judge Lee Garrett in September, he explained that he had made restitution on the bad checks he wrote. His attorney explained that William had a job in Phoenix and was married. His marriage to Kitty had been part of his good citizen

Genoa Kathleen "Kitty" Smyth Voorhis's mausoleum marker next to that of her mother, Myrtle Johnson Smyth Puckett. *Author's collection.*

defense. William's attorney worked out a deal for him. The judge placed Raisor on probation.

Just weeks before their first wedding anniversary in May 1959, Kitty sued William for divorce. Not to be outdone, William sued Kitty for divorce in February 1960.

In the following years, Kitty's mother, Myrtle, remarried, and Kitty stayed single, discarding the Raisor name and returning to use the Voorhis name. Kitty died on Christmas Day 1987.

Myrtle brought Kitty's remains back to Southwest Virginia. Kitty is entombed in a mausoleum in Abingdon, and her mother joined her eleven years later. As in life, in death, Myrtle was her daughter's one true companion.

Kitty's appeal to Jimmy, when they first met in Oak Ridge, ignited the events that caused Jimmy to stop in Abingdon to visit her. Her restlessness—moving from one location to another—opened the door for Jimmy to stay at the Clark boardinghouse.

5

THE MODEL FAMILY/SON NEXT DOOR

ANDREW SUMMERS

Andrew Rowan Summers was born on December 15, 1912, to Lewis Preston (L.P.) Summers and Anne Katherine "Annie Kate" Barbee Summers. Andrew had six living siblings: Gay White (eleven), Jane Douglas (nine), Lewis Preston Jr. (eight), Katherine B. (seven), John Grant (six) and Fannie (three). A few months after Andrew was born, his sister Fannie died at the age of four.

L.P. and Annie Kate welcomed a baby girl on June 13, 1914. Olivia Wirt Summers, just eighteen months younger than Andrew, seemed to have a special bond with her brother. Maybe that connection was forged because the next living sibling closest in age to Andrew was John, who was six years older.

By the time Andrew and Olivia were teenagers, the other siblings had left the home. In 1930, seventeen-year-old Andrew and fifteen-year-old Olivia had little use for their neighbors' children. Little Hal Clark was only six, Dorothy was a two-year-old toddler and Nancy was not quite a year old.

As rambunctious as Little Hal was, Andrew and Olivia were his opposites. As the last two children in the home, their mother in her early fifties and father in his early sixties, Andrew and Olivia seemed more like adults than teens.

Andrew's father, L.P., was a well-known and respected attorney in the region and one of the most successful trial lawyers in the state of Virginia. He also collected and wrote the stories of the area, preserving Southwest Virginia history more than any other person in his time. Andrew headed to

Left: Andrew and Olivia Summers at their home on East Valley Street, next door to the Clark home, around 1930. *Historical Society of Washington County, Virginia.*

Below, left to right: Eddie Mead (a friend of Andrew), Olivia Summers and Andrew Summers, 1938. *Historical Society of Washington County, Virginia.*

the University of Virginia in Charlottesville to pursue his law degree. His goal was to work alongside his father.

With an innate musical talent, Andrew loved the folk music he heard growing up in the Appalachian Highlands region, and he began collecting ballads and learned to play the dulcimer.

At the University of Virginia (UVA), Andrew developed his singing skills with the Glee Club. There, he met architecture student William "Bill" Robert Stephenson. Bill Stephenson was from Norfolk, Virginia. Andy and Bill may have been from opposite corners of the state, but they both loved the performing arts. Along with singing together in Glee Club (Bill a baritone and Andy a tenor), they were part of the recently formed student group the Virginia Players, dedicated to producing plays for the university and surrounding community.

The following summer, Andy visited Bill Stephenson at Willoughby Beach in Norfolk and convinced his friend to come to Abingdon with him for a few days. While in Abingdon, Bill explored the area with Andy, attended parties with both Andy and Olivia and learned the history and architecture of the town from L.P. before he returned to Norfolk. Andy and Bill were friends for many years.

Andy returned to Charlottesville and UVA. The university created an idyllic environment for Andy. The young man pursued his studies, music, theater and campus life. The Depression gripping the country had little effect on the students. Andy and Bill were smart, talented and handsome young men—making them some of the most popular students at the university. During the Depression—just like today—family money wasn't a prerequisite of admiration and social success at UVA, but it didn't hurt.

The next summer, Andy spent a week with Bill Stephenson at Virginia Beach. The young men moved to the coveted rooms of the Lawn at UVA that fall. Andy lived at 45 West Lawn, and Bill lived at 41 West Lawn. The university described the distinction of the rooms: "It is considered an honor to live in one of the University's prestigious rooms on the Lawn, probably the most popular place for all UVA students to relax, study and play. Located in Mr. Jefferson's original buildings, the Academical Village, these 54 single rooms are truly in the center of the University."

In December 1934, Andrew passed the state bar exam. That Christmas, Andrew and Olivia returned to Abingdon to spend the holiday with their parents. Andrew's friends didn't live in Abingdon, and his siblings had moved away from the area, so when he graduated and started practicing law with his father, Andrew's restlessness emerged in his other pursuits. He enjoyed history, like his historian father, but Andy had a tactile interest in antique furniture, décor, fabrics and architecture.

His college friend Bill Stephenson moved to New York City after graduation, not to follow his architecture degree but to live his twenties out as a dance instructor for Arthur Murray. His dancing expanded into teaching contracts in Hawaii and Los Angeles.

By the end of the 1930s, Andrew had moved to Manhattan as well. Andrew and Bill had a great time as bachelors in the West Village.

While in Los Angeles, Bill met a girl named Patricia Ziegfeld. She was Hollywood royalty. Patricia's mother was actress Billie Burke, best known today as Glinda, the good witch, in *The Wizard of Oz* movie. Patricia's father was Broadway's and Hollywood's Florenz Ziegfeld Jr. The young couple made their home in Los Angeles, where Bill Stephenson became a leading architect for celebrity homes.

Andrew lived at 181 Waverly Place in Greenwich Village. At twenty-seven, he worked for a law firm and was a law editor for Frank Shepard Company. He sang at churches and later became a musician and singer of Appalachian folk music at festivals and on NBC Radio.

When Olivia married Howard Jackson Dutcher in October 1942 at Sinking Spring Presbyterian Church in Abingdon, Andrew brought his domestic partner to the wedding. Olivia insisted that both Andrew and his partner, Renato d'Onofrio, serve as ushers in her wedding.

The two young men moved to a larger apartment in the Village at 24 West Tenth Street. Back in Abingdon, Andrew and Renato frequently visited L.P. and Annie Kate at their homeplace on Valley Street. The family seemed to welcome Andrew's domestic partner, as did his work associates and friends in Abingdon and the surrounding areas.

Andrew and Renato, in 1945, met Jimmy Newton, who was boarding at the Clark home in Abingdon, next door to the Summerses' home on Valley Street.

6

THE SNOWSTORM

ABINGDON, VIRGINIA
DECEMBER 1944

MONDAY, DECEMBER 11, 1944

Cold wind whipped across the Midwest and Upper Mississippi Valley of the United States and turned the rain to snow. By the afternoon, the Bristol Virginia Police reported five inches of snow and slush on the streets with the threat of a layer of ice forming across the region. The wind drifted the snow deeper in places along and over the roads. By the next day, ten inches of snow had accumulated as the storm continued. The Greyhound and Fuller bus lines canceled their schedules.

Jimmy Newton sat by the frosty window of his bus and watched the snow blur the landscape. Most of the passengers had abandoned the bus in Bristol to find accommodations for the evening or for the next few days. The driver told the remaining steadfast travelers that he would go as far north as Highway 11 would allow him. His goal was to reach Wytheville by dark, but he'd have to radio ahead to check the conditions.

"This bus has weight on her side," the driver said to Jimmy. He and the other three hopeful passengers had moved to the front of the bus to watch the road as the bus churned along the highway. The big man reminded Jimmy of his father—if his father had been a blue-collar man and not a behind-the-desk man that he'd been for years. The desk chair and driver's seat caused a man to get thick and slow. Jimmy wanted to avoid that. Even with his war wounds, he tried to stay active. At each stop of the bus, he walked around the station before the trip continued. His hip and leg cramped from sitting too long. Aspirin didn't work to ease the pain. His mother insisted that rubbing Viavi cerate on his spine, hip and legs would induce a reaction with his nerves and tissues and then seep into his blood to rebuild and correct his injured body. He found the only thing the ointment healed was his loneliness when dreams woke him in the dark of night. The bus slid, but the driver recovered with a jerk of the wheel. "Folks," he said, "we're going to have to park her at the terminal in Abingdon. There's a couple of hotels around the station."

Jimmy's plan had been to stop in Abingdon for just a night. Kitty Smyth lived there—at least she did when he received his last letter from the vivacious girl. He thought they would have a few laughs, maybe several drinks. He really wasn't interested in her romantically. They had necked. He had run his hand up her skirt because she'd placed it at the top of her stockings, as if for him to experience the strength of the snaps that held the nylons in place. She giggled. He feigned respect for her as a young lady and withdrew. When he told his parents he was planning to stop to see Kitty as a detour from his trip to Manhattan, they both seemed pleased by his interest in the girl.

The pallid light of the snowy afternoon dimmed the farms along the highway. A moderate hill, an incline the passengers wouldn't have noticed without the ice, skated the bus's tires toward a ditch on the right. The skill of the driver straightened the climb, and the wheels caught traction. An older woman raised her gloved hand above her dark felt hat and cried out, "Praise Jesus!" Her husband nodded his agreement. Jimmy glanced two rows back at the other passenger who made up their foursome out of Bristol. The middle-aged businessman rubbed his wire-rimmed glasses with his handkerchief. He smiled at Jimmy and added, "Thank God—and Greyhound." The elderly woman cocked her nose up in indignation, refusing to look back at the man. Her husband grinned.

The view out the windshield went from farms to warehouses, cinderblock buildings to brick storefronts. The bus turned onto Wall Street by the warm glow of lights at the Hotel Belmont, and then the driver pulled up by Norfolk and Western Railway's passenger depot and the bus station. "Hotel Abingdon is over there," the driver said as he motioned to his left. "Good food for dinner. Check back here tomorrow to see if our buses are moving. Taxi stand is on the corner. Those boys may be driving around town before sunset, but walking is your best bet. Good luck, folks."

Digging through his suitcase once he was in the station, Jimmy found the letter from Kitty with her address. She rented a room on Valley Street from a widow and her young children. He secured a taxi ride to the address about a mile away. He thought about walking, but the deep snow would have ruined his good shoes and soaked his feet.

"A heavy snowstorm came up during the trip, and when the bus arrived in Abingdon, the roads were so bad it was impossible to continue the trip," Jimmy's mother, Edythe Newton, told a reporter. "Jimmy called us and told us he was marooned in Abingdon, stating that he could not go on to New York nor get home. He had met a young lady with whom he had corresponded who lived at the Clark home while attending school."

The taxi dropped him at the Clark house at 407 East Valley Street. The impressive house had a long front porch perched directly at the edge of the sidewalk. Concrete steps with stone pillars and iron gates flanked each side of the porch and led visitors up to the front door. Large windows trimmed with stained glass stretched from the floor to the ceiling of the front rooms. Jimmy felt odd about not calling first, but he did not have the boardinghouse owner's name to give to the telephone operator. He knocked on the door, ready to greet Kitty, but instead, a blond girl of about seven years answered.

"You selling something, mister?" she asked.

"No. I'm here to see Kitty Smyth."

"You must plan on staying a while since you brought that luggage," she said and jerked her chin at the suitcase Jimmy had set down on the porch.

"Is there someone older at home that I can talk to?"

"For your information, Mr. Luggage, I'll be eight on Friday." She turned toward the staircase behind her and yelled, "Dorothy, Kitty's got a man here to see her!" She looked at Jimmy. "Get on in the door. We're letting the heat out."

Jimmy lost his breath as one of the most beautiful girls he'd ever seen skipped down the stairs. A blond bombshell of a teenager stopped behind the little girl. "Don't yell through the house, Frances. It's unrefined." Frances stomped off. "Excuse her," Dorothy said, "she's excited by the snow and her birthday."

"On Friday," Jimmy added.

"Yes." Dorothy smiled. "I regret to inform you that Kitty has moved."

A thin woman, dressed in black, walked up behind Dorothy. "How do you do? I'm Mrs. Clark. Kitty moved to another boardinghouse, but she's still in town." She glanced out the window of the parlor. "You can't go out again in this weather. With Kitty gone, we have a furnished room to let if you need accommodations for the night."

Behind the woman, Jimmy saw a desk and bookcase near the back door under the stairs with tennis rackets and other athletic gear huddled around them. There must be a brother here, he thought. Kitty had told him Mrs. Clark was a widow. "I would appreciate the room for the night," he said. "The bus isn't running, so I'm a visitor to your fine town for a little while." He picked up his suitcase as the widow began leading him to the stairs. She stopped and regarded his slight limp. The cold and damp caused his injury to ache.

"Were you in the war?" she asked.

"Yes, ma'am. I was injured at Guadalcanal in the Pacific."

A gasp caught in Mrs. Clark's throat. Her hand went to her mouth. "Excuse me," she managed to say before escaping to the parlor.

Dorothy made no apology for her mother. "I'll show you the room and where you can freshen up before dinner." The stairs landed at a back hallway before continuing to the second floor of the front of the house. She led him to that corridor, lined on the right by windows that looked toward the neighbor's home, and to the left was a door to a low-ceilinged bedroom before the bathroom at the end of the hall. An iron bed sat to the right of the window that looked west. A wardrobe and chest of drawers cornered the room to the left of the window.

He placed his suitcase at the foot of the bed. "This is grand. Did I upset your mother with talk of the war?" But as he said it, he realized that the male presence that lingered in the house must be for a son still at war. "Your brother? Is he serving?"

Dorothy squared her shoulders and took a breath. "Little Hal was killed a year ago, four days before Thanksgiving, in Bougainville in the Solomon Islands."

"I'm so sorry." That was all he could say. He'd lost friends. He had almost died and struggled with a wounded hip.

As supper was set in the dining room, he met the other daughter, Nancy. The three daughters were Dorothy, age sixteen; Nancy, age fifteen; and Frances, seven—soon to be eight. The girls were all pretty, just like their mother. Mrs. Clark's sadness acted as a veil over her. The girls went about their chores without paying much attention to her. She sat in a rocker by the fireplace, isolated.

"How do you know Kitty?" Dorothy asked once they settled at the table for their meal.

Jimmy didn't want to get into too much discussion about Kitty, since he had little he could say about the girl besides their fondling of each other. She had tired of him. "We met outside of Knoxville in a place called Oak Ridge." He told them about graduating from KMI and enrolling in the

University of Kentucky. He explained he was traveling to a basketball game in New York City.

"Little Hal went to Virginia Polytechnic Institute to study engineering," Frances said. Nancy shot her a glaring look, as if she had mentioned a sore subject. Mrs. Clark set her fork on her plate and kept her eyes down.

Dorothy passed Jimmy the plate of biscuits. "What is your field of study?"

"I always liked athletics. Since my injury, I can't play. I'm interested in medicine. Spending months in the hospital got me curious about how we work. KMI holds its winter semester at the Florida campus, so I was on the Gulf Coast. We had classes in physiology, the study of the human body's mechanics. We would analyze each other swimming or running or just walking on the beach versus walking on the sidewalk."

Mrs. Clark looked up. "We would winter in New Smyrna. How I loved our time there. Hal and the children would spend the day at the stables with the horses or at the racetrack."

"Oh," Nancy interrupted. "You're the boy who invited Kitty to the dance down there."

Heat rushed to his cheeks. He had written to Kitty to attend the spring dance. She refused. Jimmy had been one of the older boys at KMI, since he had left high school to join the U.S. Marines. He wanted to show the younger boys that he had a steady girl, which he didn't—not that the other cadets had girlfriends in Florida. Most of the dates to the dance were local girls. The invitation had been a silly request to make to a girl so far away—and one so fickle. "That was a long way for her to go for a dance," he said. "There were plenty of girls already there." He hadn't taken a girl. He and some other boys went stag and had a magnificent time sneaking rum on the beach.

The snow continued to fall, and temperatures remained in the twenties. He had wanted to visit Clarke Beetlestone's parents in New Jersey on his trip to Manhattan and the basketball game, but all that had been canceled with the weather. He wondered what Clarke was doing at that moment in the South Pacific. Jimmy sledded down a snow-covered hill with three girls, while his best friend—yes, Beet was his dearest friend—battled the rainy season of the islands. Before he'd left Kentucky, he'd written to Beet in the hope the mail might make it. Then he found a picture postcard of Abingdon at a drugstore and sent it to Beet. He also sent one to Mr. and Mrs. Beetlestone to make his apologies for not visiting them due to the snowstorm.

The Associated Press had picked up the reporting of the road conditions in Virginia. Ice remained on many of the secondary roads throughout the state.

Friday brought Frances's birthday. The wind and snow had subsided. People ventured out again. Dorothy went to the service station to help Mr. Ropp and her uncle C.M. adjust tire chains, top off antifreeze and generally winterize their neighbors' automobiles. Many had been caught unprepared by the early storm.

Nancy traveled down the street to let Kitty know Jimmy was in town and staying in her old room at the Clark home. Kitty and Nancy walked into the Clark house just as Frances and her friends rushed out to the Zephyr Theatre for a showing of *The Centerville Ghost* and a celebration of her birthday.

When Kitty saw Jimmy, she didn't smile. "What a surprise," she said. "I didn't know you were going to visit."

He told her about the trip to Madison Square Garden for the basketball game and the snowstorm stranding him in Abingdon. "How's about going to a movie tonight?" he asked.

She glanced around the parlor. Mrs. Clark and Nancy had gone into the kitchen to give them privacy, but Kitty knew they could hear every word they said. "I have plans with my girlfriends. If I had known you were making a stop here, I would have cleared some time. But," she said and took a deep breath, "I'm busy."

Mrs. Clark stormed into the room. "You, young lady, go to a movie with this boy. He made a trip just to surprise you. He's a veteran. You show some appreciation for his service."

"I thank you to mind your business and allow me to mind mine," Kitty shot back. "You are not my mother. I do as I please." Then she said to Jimmy, "Grab your coat. Let's go out on the sidewalk to talk in private."

The Ropp and Clark Filling Station at Main and Tanner Streets during the blizzard of December 1944. *David Patton.*

Once outside, they settled next door at the L.P. Summers's house by its front garden wall, away from the view of the Clark's parlor window. "Why did you come here?" Kitty asked. "I'm going on adventures. I want to see other places. I don't want a steady boyfriend." She paused and stared Jimmy in the eyes. "You don't want a steady girl."

"Maybe I do and maybe I don't. If the right girl came along—" he looked away from Kitty's inquisitive eyes. "That Dorothy is a real looker."

"She's way too young for you." Kitty touched the sleeve of his coat. "There's no hurry for you to find a wife. Mrs. Clark is right. You have served all of us in the marines. Your injury—how is your hip?"

"Acts up. Hurts like hell." He turned away from her. "I took Anacin, BC, Nebs or any aspirin I could find. I rubbed my hip with Ben-Gay and Aspirub and my mother's Viavi cerate wonder drug. It's all shit. In the hospital, they gave me morphine. That dulled the pain. I can't get it outside the hospital. Whiskey helps."

Kitty withdrew a cigarette case from her handbag. She snapped it open and pulled out a hand-rolled cigarette. Jimmy fished in his pocket for his Zippo, found it and flipped it aflame. She inhaled to light the cigarette and then handed it to Jimmy. "Take a toke of my friend Mary Jane."

He pulled her off the sidewalk and to the driveway of the Summerses's house. "Damn, Kit. You smoke a reefer on the street?"

"No one is around. Mr. Summers died last year. Mrs. Summers spends time with her daughter in South Carolina. The house is usually empty unless Andrew comes home from New York with his special friend." She took the joint from him, inhaled and winked. "When Andy comes home, that's when we have parties."

He accepted the joint back from her and snuck a look at the large, unoccupied house.

"I might be able to get some morphine from friends in Bristol. In the meantime, take these." She handed him the cigarette case. "They'll help ease some of the pain—can't hurt." She pecked his cheek with a kiss. "I'm not the person for you." With that, she walked back down Valley Street.

SUNDAY, DECEMBER 17, 1944

Jimmy tried to control the effects of his PTSD while around other people. He found alcohol an effective coping mechanism that was fairly socially acceptable. He experienced tremors in his legs that he would overcome by tapping his foot on the floor or bouncing his knee like an adolescent boy trapped in a schoolroom. Loud noises like an automobile backfiring caused him to flatten himself against the nearest wall. During a conversation with Mrs. Clark and the girls, he realized his mind had blanked out and lost the thread of the discussion. Any psychological affliction was a taboo subject for men at the time. Even among other veterans Jimmy had met in the hospital, they never discussed emotional or mental health. Clarke Beetlestone had been the only man Jimmy confided in since they'd been together during their first front-line battles.

On Sunday, the Clark women dressed for church and invited Jimmy to attend with them. He wasn't an ardent churchgoer, but he loved the music.

When Helen heard Jimmy sing, she gripped the pew in front of her to steady herself. He sang like an angel. Tears filled her eyes. Thoughts of Hal, her mother and her father—all ripped from her life in eight short months—and then the loss of Little Hal just over a year later left her feeling abandoned. The blues grabbed her and wouldn't let go. The girls needed her. But she needed Hal and her parents. Why was she left alone? With Jimmy standing next to her and the girls on her other side, she felt like they were a ragtag family. The hymn rolled into the chorus, and Jimmy's voice filled with strength. She couldn't stop the tears. Nancy must have noticed, because she handed her mother a handkerchief. Helen set her hymnal in the rack and dabbed her eyes. To her shock, she realized she had reached over to hold Jimmy's hand. She let go, and he nodded to her with a smile. She hoped the other parishioners hadn't seen her indiscretion. This was the congregation of her parents, her in-laws, Hal's friends and associates and Little Hal and the girls' schoolmates and teachers. But for the first time in over four years, she felt like she had a family again.

While leaving the church, Helen approached M.H. Musser, who was to be the master of ceremonies for that Friday's Teenage Canteen. She offered Jimmy as a musical guest to perform at the Christmas cabaret–themed party. Jimmy had not planned to stay in town much longer. He had played the piano for Mrs. Clark and the girls after their suppers. He loved to perform, since it took his mind away. Mr. Musser extended an invitation to him to be part of the cabaret. Dorothy and Nancy encouraged him. He glanced at Mrs. Clark and saw her smiling, a rare occurrence. He agreed to be part of the entertainment.

At the Friday evening event, Mr. Musser introduced Jimmy as "the guest of Mrs. Hal Clark," and Jimmy played selections of standards, current favorites and Christmas songs on the piano for the energetic teens and chaperones.

The Abingdon railroad passenger station in the 1940s. *Historical Society of Washington County, Virginia.*

SATURDAY, DECEMBER 23, 1944

Jimmy knew he needed to return to Kentucky by that Monday for Christmas. Mrs. Clark presented a proposition to him as he packed his clothes: drive her and the girls to New Smyrna, Florida, for the winter. Spending the winter in Florida appealed to Jimmy. The snowstorm that had stranded him two weeks earlier was all the winter he cared to have. Plus, the sun and ocean would be good for his hip. And Florida held fun and adventure and young men and women his age. The thoughts invigorated him.

A train back to Kentucky had Jimmy with his parents by Christmas Day. He informed them of the hospitality of Mrs. Clark and her offer to hire him to drive the family to Florida, a place his mother and father knew he enjoyed. By January 1, 1945, Jimmy had boarded a train in Louisville and arrived at the Abingdon train station.

7

THE GOOD TIMES

NEW SMYRNA, FLORIDA
WINTER/SPRING 1945

The drive from Abingdon to New Smyrna Beach, Florida, in 1945 probably consisted of a thirteen- to fourteen-hour trek across state highways. A halfway point—had they wanted to break up the journey—was their usual stop at the Barbara Hutton plantation south of Charleston. Time to see the horses and friends would have been a welcome respite. They probably didn't stay more than a night, since Jimmy loved to drive and they were all looking forward to the warm beaches of Florida.

The girls always enrolled in school while they spent the winter in Florida, and they did so again in the winter of 1945. Helen settled the family into the cottage they rented, unpacking and attempting to get the girls into a routine. They rented a house in the old Coronado Beach section of New Smyrna.

By mid-January, a newspaper article alerted the local residents that Jimmy would take over the Ideal Laundry truck route. This was steady work for him and an opportunity to meet people. He made connections with the resorts and clubs and booked several musical gigs. The March 10 edition of the *Daytona Beach Morning Journal* announced that he was "the new piano artist at the B. and T." The "B. and T." refers to the popular Bath and Tennis Club, a ritzy country club for the elite of the Daytona Beach area. From the morning paper's March 13 edition: "It was a big evening for the boogie with pianist Jimmy Newton in the [Bath and Tennis Club] lounge." Jimmy and his boogie piano had found a home in Florida. As a young, handsome, twenty-one-year-old ex-marine, Jimmy probably

The Barbara Hutton Plantation at Willtown Bluff, Yonges Island, South Carolina; postcard. *University of South Carolina, South Caroliniana Library.*

had his pick of dates from the clientele of the Bath and Tennis Club, as well as from the staff and other musicians.

This time in Florida was Jimmy's heyday. He was young and popular, surrounded by his musical peers, and he made money from his truck route for the laundry and from his music. Just like he had the previous winter at the Kentucky Military Institute's Gulf Coast campus—but without the faculty supervision, intense studying and routine classes—Jimmy spent his free time in the sand and surf with his friends. His beach nights may have been filled with music, drinks and casual sexual conquests, but his days included driving the laundry truck and embarking on civic service activities.

The Sea Scouts, a part of the Boy Scouts of America focused on boating, navigation and competitive regattas, recruited Jimmy to help start a Sea Scout "ship," the term for a troop. The Sea Scouts, in the 1940s, were for young men aged fourteen to twenty. Jimmy's marine background and his age made him an ideal skipper, or leader of the group.

During Jimmy's immersion into the social scene of New Smyrna Beach, Helen became lonely with the girls in school. Her and Hal's previous excursions to the stables, tracks and horse shows in the area wouldn't have held the same allure alone as they had when she was with her beloved husband.

Early May 1945 became a time of celebration for veterans, serving military members and citizens of the United States with turning points in World War II. Germany surrendered, and May 8 was declared Victory in Europe Day, or V-E Day. The welcome news lifted the mood of the nation. The European victory invigorated the military and citizens around Florida. Interest turned toward the Pacific battles. Jimmy and the Clark family looked to the South Pacific, where the U.S. Navy and Marines had sacrificed so much.

The Sea Scouts gained sponsorship from the American Legion, which Jimmy joined the same evening. The first event the Sea Scouts tackled was a social and informal dance at the Masonic temple. "Proceeds will go to purchase later a small ship for Sea Scout work," explained the *Daytona Beach News-Journal*.

By May, the girls had finished their semester at school, and Helen was prepared to return to Abingdon.

Jimmy was not ready to leave Florida.

As was his commitment, Jimmy drove the Clarks to Abingdon but turned around and took the train back to New Smyrna Beach. Jimmy continued with his pickup and delivery with the laundry service and his music gigs at the local resorts and community events, and he continued as the skipper of the newly formed Sea Scouts.

In Abingdon, the Clark girls stayed with their father's brother Ed Clark, while Helen; her brother, C.M.; and his wife, Louise, traveled to Louisville and Churchill Downs for the Kentucky Derby on June 9.

Helen wanted to visit Jimmy's parents. C.M. drove her and Louise to Anchorage, a suburb east of Louisville. Mrs. Newton answered the door and welcomed them in. The home seemed large for the older couple, Helen thought as she smiled at the portly woman in a plain shirtwaist dress with little pale daisies scattered across the cotton fabric. Jimmy said his mother had just turned sixty. To Helen's surprise, behind Mrs. Newton stood a younger woman with a squirming toddler. This must be the sister, Mabel, Helen thought as she smiled at the woman. With their introductions made, Helen found that Mabel's husband was out that Sunday afternoon, but Mr. Newton was home. He joined the group in the front parlor. He didn't look a thing like Jimmy. Where Jimmy was handsome, well-built and crackling with personality, Mr. Newton seemed sluggish in every sense of the word. Maybe he had too much to drink during the Derby yesterday, like C.M. Helen looked back at her brother, who was leaning against the piano by the window.

C.M.'s wife, Louise, hit it off with Mrs. Newton. They chatted about her home, her grandchild—a boy named James—and the late-spring flowers that made Kentucky so brilliant in June. C.M. didn't say much. Helen felt she had nothing in common with this family except Jimmy.

"As I mentioned on the phone," Helen began, "our family has become quite fond of Jimmy, and we're impressed with his work ethic. I think there's a future for him with the Ropp and Clark Filling Station. Since my husband passed and Mr. Ropp concentrates more on the electrical contracting business, C.M. could use a young man at the station."

Mrs. Newton looked at her husband. "Emmett, didn't Jimmy have other plans once he recovered from his war wounds?"

Emmett Newton seemed startled to be called on to join the conversation. "Why, yes, I think Jim talked of getting into the medical profession."

Mabel jumped in. "Jimmy is so talented with his music. I know he wants to pursue that. I'm not sure a filling station would be something he'd enjoy." She bounced the toddler on her knee. "A young man like my brother has a variety of choices. He'd have more opportunity around Louisville."

C.M. pulled out the piano bench and settled there. "He's just twenty-one years old and has plenty of time to decide on his life's work."

"Actually, tomorrow is his birthday," Mrs. Newton added.

"I mailed him a lovely present—something he can use in Florida," Helen said. "A Jantzen blue swimsuit with a white belt."

Mrs. Newton and Mabel exchanged looks. Emmett Newton frowned. "He may be turning twenty-two and a war veteran, but Jim is still our boy, and we'd like him to come home," Emmett said.

"Kentucky is a beautiful place," Louise said. "Virginia is nice, as well. Jimmy really likes Abingdon. He should spend time there this summer with plenty of hunting and fishing to do. It's not as urban as here. The outdoors would be good for him." She glanced at C.M.

C.M. added, "Bottom line, Emmett—and I can tell you're a bottom line kind of man—my nephew, Helen's son, Hal Jr., was killed in the Pacific. We all thought Hal Jr. would take over the family business. Now, his little sister, Dorothy, is working with me at the station. Prettiest girl you will ever see, that Dorothy. The filling station is no place for a girl. We get plenty of boys stopping in to see her, but they don't have money to get their cars fixed. Jimmy's a good man. He has expressed interest in learning about cars. He could work with us, have a good family to board with." He nodded to Helen. "Keep him out of the trouble that a lot of young veterans get into when they have spare time on their hands. We'd appreciate you encouraging him to work with us for a little while. It would be good for him."

Eventually, Mr. Newton agreed that a steady job away from the Florida beach could benefit Jimmy. He said he would urge Jimmy to talk to Helen about staying with her and the girls while he worked at the filling station.

In Florida that same day, June 10, the Sunday edition of the *Daytona Beach News-Journal* announced that Jimmy was to appear at the chamber of commerce dinner to play the piano and lead the group in a sing-along. He lived his best life that spring. The next day, Monday, June 11, 1945, Jimmy celebrated his twenty-second birthday with his Sea Scouts in the ocean waves, and then, later in the evening, he met his friends and other navy and marine veterans on the beach for a roaring bonfire. They celebrated with adult drinks and enjoyed being young and worry-free.

One of Jimmy's Sea Scouts was young Breece McCray. At the time, Breece was fourteen years old and fascinated with his Sea Scouts skipper. After all, Jimmy Newton had visited New York City and the World's Fair, joined the marines after Pearl Harbor and fought in the jungles of Guadalcanal. He could also bang out boogie piano that rivaled the players at bars near Bethune Beach and then switch to a sweet Rogers and Hammerstein tune or a Chopin piano concerto.

The next decade, Breece McCray was elected to New Smyrna Beach's city commission and became the city's youngest mayor. But in 1945, he was a young boy who idolized Jimmy Newton.

On Saturday, June 30, 1945, Jimmy received word that his father was ill. The news must have been conveyed seriously, since he left the next day, Sunday, July 1, on the train, accompanied by his young friend Breece, bound for Anchorage, Kentucky.

In Kentucky, Jimmy found his father recovering from a heart attack. The doctors warned Emmett about taking his work stress home and not getting enough exercise. Edythe and Mabel worried over him. Jimmy promised he would be there when his father needed him. Maybe Florida was too far away from his ailing father.

Young Breece McCray returned to New Smyrna Beach on the train while Jimmy stayed in Anchorage. Mabel and her toddler son, James, rode with Jimmy to take Breece to the train station. On the way back to the house, Mabel had more bad news for Jimmy.

Jimmy steered his father's four-door, gray Chevrolet sedan through the streets of Louisville. Mabel balanced little James on her knee, where he kept reaching for the gear stick. "He's growing fast," Jimmy said of baby James.

man who is employed there . . . Jimmy Newton and Breece McCray will leave today for Anchorage, Ky., called by the illness of Jimmy's father . . . **Ensign Donald Perry of Ft. Pierce is the weekend guest of**

(WRITE NOTHING ABOVE THIS LINE)

MUSTER ROLL OF OFFICERS AND ENLISTED MEN OF THE U. S. MARINE CORPS
PRISONERS OF WAR AND MISSING PERSONS DETACHMENT, HQ., U. S. MARINE CORPS
FROM _____ 1 January _____ , TO _____ 31 January _____ , 19 45 , INCLUSIVE

NO.	NAME AND RANK	ENLISTED	REMARKS
1	ABRAHAM, Edwin A.	B	
2	ADAMS, Oliver R.	B	
3	ALBERT, Charles E.	B	
4	ALLEN, Lavern K.	B	
5	ALVARADO, Baldwin C., Jr.	A	
6	ANDERSON, Ralph W.	A	
7	ANDERSON, Robert L.	A	
8	BAKEWELL, Charles H.	C	(AVN)
9	BARRETT, Robert E.	B	
10	BARTELME, Herbert E.	A	
11	BAUM, Robert A.	C	(AVN)
12	BEETLESTONE, Leslie C.	372380	5, jdfr H&S, 11Prov, 155mm GunBn, FMF. Missing in Action since 5Nov44.
13	BERTHEAUD, Lionel A.	A	

Top: Daytona Beach News Journal's July 1, 1945 mention of Jimmy and Breece rushing to Kentucky because of Emmett Newton's heart attack. *Newsbank/Daytona Beach Florida Regional Library.*

Bottom: The muster roll of the U.S. Marine Corps (January 1945) showing Leslie Clarke Beetlestone, missing in action (MIA) since November 5, 1944. *National Archives at Washington, D.C.*

"I'm so relieved that Father is doing better and will see his grandson grow up." Mabel drew the child close to her and rocked him. The restraint only emboldened the toddler to squirm more. "I—" she started. "Jim, pull over to that parking lot, please."

When he saw the serious look on her face, he asked, "What's up?"

"You received a letter from New Jersey a couple of months ago. I knew it couldn't be good. Father said to forward it to you in Florida, but Mother and I thought we'd give it to you in person." She fidgeted with the baby's jumper. "After Father had his heart attack and I knew you were coming home, I opened the letter—to know if it was really bad news." She took a breath. "Your friend Clarke Beetlestone was—"

"MIA," Jimmy finished for her. "In November. Probably in a prisoner of war camp."

"No. He's dead." She didn't know any other way to convey the awful fact. "His parents wanted you to know."

He couldn't breathe. His nose began to drip, and his eyes flooded.

Mabel scooted over to Jimmy and put an arm around his shoulders. She held both her brother and son tight as their protector and source of strength—at least for that moment.

Emmett recovered and returned home from the hospital. Edythe and Mabel fussed over him. Mabel's husband, Lem, and little James tried to entertain Jimmy, but Jimmy felt restless.

He received a letter from Helen Clark inquiring about his father and his plans for the summer. She and C.M. had a job for him at the service station. A week later, she telephoned his parent's house. His mother, reluctantly, suggested that working in Virginia would be more convenient than working in Florida, in case she or his father might need him.

The prospects of being closer to his family and that the Clarks spent their winters at New Smyrna Beach made the job in Abingdon seem like a good solution, at least for the near future. Jimmy's previous ideas for the end of the war had included moving to Manhattan with Beet. Now, those plans had disappeared in the Japanese gunfire of the South Pacific.

8

SETTLING IN AS BROTHER/SON/LOVER

ABINGDON, VIRGINIA, SUMMER 1945

Jimmy arrived back in Abingdon on July 16 or 17. There is no record of him returning to New Smyrna Beach to retrieve his belongings, say goodbye to his friends and Sea Scouts or wrap up his professional or personal business. The facts about Jimmy Newton support the conclusion that he was emotionally attached to his friends and acquaintances. The opposite could be determined with the introduction of his shell shock; he might have cut ties and moved on. The effects of the war and his upbringing mixed together tended to either put him into a puppy mode of bonding to people or a lone wolf mode of detaching from others.

"Personalities change with PTSD [post-traumatic stress disorder]," explained Major General Rodney D. Fogg, (retired) U.S. Army. "They called it shell shock back then. People thought a person could just get over the 'shock.' Well, you're not going to get over it. It's with you forever." Major General Fogg described a person with PTSD as possibly having times of being their old self and other times of struggling with their memories. Jimmy seemed to cut ties with his Florida friends, and he began creating new friendships in Abingdon.

Jimmy continued to play the role of the dutiful son to his parents and the role of friend to the Clark family—after all, they had lost Hal Jr. They needed him to fill that void. At times, he couldn't set his focus on his life. Who was he? What should he be to the people around him? He probably felt he'd left the real Jimmy in the Pacific and that this Jimmy would mold to

An eastern view Main Street, 1940s. *Historical Society of Washington County, Virginia.*

what people expected of him. That would be easier than trying to mine the depths of his heart to find who he really was.

C.M. Talbert brought Jimmy into the Ropp and Clark Filling Station, a block from Helen's house, to help with their business.

Jimmy understood the workings of an engine. He'd been trained by the U.S. Marines at Parris Island in the motor pool and as a truck driver. C.M. and Dorothy taught Jimmy all he needed to know about servicing the station's customers. C.M. made sure everyone knew he was in charge. Jimmy's manners were smooth and calming for the women customers. But C.M. could be harsh in his critiques of the job Jimmy did on piddling tasks—as Jimmy viewed them—like sweeping the garage floor and around the gas pumps or washing a customer's car after repair.

One late July afternoon, the summer heat bounced off the concrete of the service station, almost blinding Jimmy from its intensity. The midafternoon shift was the worst. C.M., luckily, had left for his usual afternoon siesta. Jimmy had had enough of C.M.'s criticism and hounding about how to do things. Dorothy was working in the back shed's garage on an oil change.

A black 1936 Studebaker Commander pulled into the filling station. Mrs. Hagy, a regular customer, asked for a fill-up. As her Studebaker was filled with gas, Jimmy cleaned her windshield and checked her tire pressure. He wrote up Mrs. Hagy's ticket. She decided to put it on her tab. Jimmy patted the fender as she drove off.

Dorothy Clark. *Gay Leonard.*

Dorothy came from the service bay, wiping her hands on a rag. She looked at the gas pump. "Mrs. Hagy—or, more likely, Mr. Hagy—will be back soon."

"Why's that?"

She reached up and grabbed a car's gas cap. "Here. You forgot to put it back on. Don't let Uncle C. know. He'll chew you out."

"Damn it! I wonder if I could catch her before she gets home."

"Uncle C. took the car," Dorothy said. "You'd have to run awfully fast to overtake Mrs. Hagy. She drives like the devil himself is tracking her."

When C.M. returned and Dorothy went home, Jimmy heard words spew from the man that he hadn't heard since basic training at Parris Island. He knew not to try to argue his case. The forgotten gas cap was his fault. C.M. pulled the Hagy account information and had Jimmy call them to explain his blunder and promise to drive the cap to them the next morning. That satisfied the Hagys, good church-going people. But C.M. mumbled and grumbled about it the rest of the evening and most of the next day until he found something else to blame on Jimmy.

The next evening, after the filling station was closed for the night, Jimmy saw lights on at the Summerses' house next door. He stood at the window in the hallway outside his room and stared. Yes, someone was definitely at the neighbors' house and had the windows open to the evening breeze.

Frances skipped down the stairs to the first floor. Jimmy caught her attention before she passed him. "Is Mrs. Summers back from South Carolina?" he asked.

"Naw, man," Frances said, trying out some slang she'd heard in a movie. "That's the cool cat Andy and his man Renato." She continued down the staircase.

Through supper, Jimmy tried to think of an excuse to go next door to meet the frequently discussed Andrew Summers. Frances brought it up first. "Mother, I see that Mr. Andrew Summers has come home to roost."

"That's disrespectful of your elders and stop that foolish talk," Helen said. "Mr. Summers is a successful attorney in New York City." She looked at Jimmy and added, "Andrew always brings me musical theatre records. He goes to the latest shows."

"Maybe I should introduce myself," Jimmy said. "I enjoyed my time in New York when I went to the World's Fair. I'd like to hear what's going on up there."

Nancy brought around plates of peach pie for their dessert. "You better go next door early. Later in the night, the crowd there is three sheets to the wind."

"Girls," Helen scolded. "That's enough slang. Watch your language, even among family."

Jimmy retired to the side porch to smoke a Lucky while the girls washed the dishes. A familiar young lady sashayed up the driveway—Kitty. Her cotton dress hugged her curves, and the way the setting sun clarified her profile, he could tell she wasn't wearing an underslip.

"What's caught your attention, marine?" she asked as she winked. She smoothed her dress and then looked over her shoulder at the Summerses' house. "Andy and Renato are here for a few days. I thought I'd stop by for a few laughs, maybe a drink or two. Come on," she said. "You need to meet some men of culture."

He snuffed out his cigarette and walked Kitty to the back porch of the house next door.

Kitty knocked on the screen door and then opened it and walked in. "Yoohoo!" she called out. "It's your favorite girl-about-town. I brought you a swoony marine."

Andrew and Renato entered the kitchen from the front room, drinks in hands. Andrew Summers looked rich with his tailored clothes and expensive shoes. Renato d'Onofrio had a mysterious, smoldering gaze like Tyrone Power. After introductions and drinks, they settled in the parlor. Jimmy told Andrew about his trip to Manhattan during the World's Fair. Kitty and Renato rolled jazz cigarettes. More young people from around town showed up, and before the sun set, a full rollicking party was underway. Kitty urged Jimmy to the piano. He and Andrew sang popular hits, starting with Perry Como's "Dig You Later (A Hubba-Hubba-Hubba)" and ending with most of the party guests crooning Billie Holiday's "Lover Man, Oh Where Can You Be?"

After going outside to cool off, Andrew asked Jimmy, "Why don't you move to Manhattan?" They stood on the back porch, sipping their whiskey.

"A buddy of mine from the marines has family near there. Our plan was to go when we were both back from the Pacific."

"You would fit well with our crowd in Greenwich Village. I could help you and your friend find day jobs, and you'll easily get gigs in night clubs. The service station probably isn't that stimulating for you," Andrew said.

"Clarke won't be coming home, MIA and presumed dead." The words caught in his throat, and he took a gulp of his drink.

Andrew looked down and shook his head. "I'm sorry. Finding a true friend in life is difficult enough without a war tearing us apart." He opened his arms and embraced Jimmy, a long and sorrowful hug.

Jimmy hadn't had a hug from a man since he had left his military brothers. It startled him at first, but he saw that no one at the party gave them a second look and relaxed. He stepped back and took a sip of his drink. "I'm here now," Jimmy said. "This is fairly close to my family in Kentucky. Maybe one day I'll make it to the big city." He grinned. "You and Renato seem to," he searched for the words and then added, "seem to be accepted by people— your close relationship, that is."

"People around here have known me all my life. I've always been me. My father and mother never made a fuss." Andrew rattled the ice in his drink. "Don't hesitate to live your life. That's what you fought for."

The Damascus "Rock School," where Jimmy Newton taught and coached. *Historical Society of Washington County, Virginia.*

Kitty walked up behind Andrew and kissed his cheek. "I'm heading home," she said. "Jim, you staying?"

"I have work tomorrow morning," Jimmy said. "I'll walk you out." He said his goodbyes to Andrew and Renato and the other people at the party.

Before she continued down the sidewalk, Kitty gave Jimmy a slip of paper with a name on it. "Go over to Damascus and talk to this teacher. She's a friend of mine and said the school needs a football coach to help build a team. You'd be good at that, and it would get you around more people your age."

Jimmy's lingering thoughts of returning to New Smyrna Beach or moving to Manhattan were shelved when he talked to the administration at the Damascus, Virginia school. The Rock School, as the locals called it, since it was built of river rock, housed both the elementary and the high school classes.

The thought of teaching and coaching invigorated Jimmy. He was team-oriented and a natural leader. It gave him purpose. The filling station wasn't a fit for him. His drinking had increased because of his dissatisfaction with working at the station, not interacting with other young men like he did in the service, keeping his life on-hold because of his father's health and, the biggest reason, Beet's death. His life would be so different, he thought, if Beet had returned from the Pacific.

HELEN KNEW JIMMY WASN'T enjoying his job at the filling station. But the work helped the family, gave him some spending money, paid the meager amount of rent she charged for his room and allowed him time to pursue his musical interests.

When Jimmy had first arrived that past December, he reminded her of Little Hal. They were both born in June 1923, both in the military in the Pacific and, amazingly to her, both served at Guadalcanal. Her daughters enjoyed Jimmy's company, and although he and Little Hal did not share all the same interests, they did have some in common. Jimmy liked cars, made friends easily and exhibited the good manners of a strict upbringing. He did not like guns. Helen knew Dorothy could out-shoot him at targets and skeet. She suspected that his hunting trips with the local boys had evolved from the original intent of genuine sportsmanship to more of a drunken weekend.

Helen saw Jimmy was restless and didn't sleep well. She had often heard him, in the middle of the night, go down the stairs and out to the side porch. She did not care for his use of alcohol. He was, after all, a grown man and would make his own decisions, as her husband, Hal, had. Her mind wrestled with the dichotomy of her view of Jimmy. At times, she felt motherly to him, while at other times, she had a peer relationship with the young man. He was wise beyond his years, surprising her with his insight into the human condition. He understood her—maybe more than Hal had. The modern men, veterans who had experienced so much during the war, related better to women, she believed. Since Hal's death, the other men of the town viewed her as a widow, their friend's widow. No one took her to dinner or out dancing. Nancy tuned to a musical program on the radio one evening, and Jimmy, to Helen's delight, stood up from his chair, walked over to Helen, bowed and asked her for a dance. He spun her around the parlor. Dorothy danced with Frances. Nancy giggled at the spectacle.

In August, one of the town council members organized a garden party at the Martha Washington Inn. Hal had been on the council with these men. Helen knew their wives. Hal's uncle James Hines had been the town's mayor twice. She heard about the garden party, not from an invitation but from Jimmy saying he would be providing musical entertainment for the event. The slight of not being invited infuriated her. If Hal had been alive, this would not have happened. Helen decided she would go as Jimmy's guest. He called it a grand idea. The tongues will be wagging, she thought with wicked delight.

The chatter network of the town included alley conversations, garden gossip and—the most efficient method—the telephone company's "party line" standard. The Inter-Mountain Telephone Company connected several households to a loop, each with its own phone number. But every home on the loop would ring when someone was called on that party line. Each home had a distinctive ring, so the neighbors knew if the call was intended for them. Many times, a person would pick up the receiver to make a call, only to be surprised by a neighbor's conversation in progress.

Nancy heard the neighbors' rumors when she attempted to call a friend. The line was in use. Before she could replace the receiver, she heard her mother's name mentioned. They talked about the scandal of Helen Clark and the young marine staying at her home. Nancy slammed down the phone to make sure the women knew they had been overheard. She didn't tell her mother or her sisters.

9

THE COACH AND THE WIDOW

ABINGDON AND DAMASCUS, VIRGINIA
FALL 1945

Jimmy met with Damascus principal S.W. Edmondson to discuss the seventh grade teaching position and the reestablishment of a high school football team with him as their coach and school athletic director. Mr. Edmondson, a serious and dedicated educator, liked Jimmy, and veterans had the support and encouragement of a grateful population. His only hesitation about Jimmy was his lack of a teaching degree or certificate. Jimmy's experience with the marines and Sea Scouts, his own good grades in school and his musical involvement with the church and civic clubs helped Mr. Edmondson petition to Washington County Schools superintendent K.P. Birckhead to issue a local teaching permit to Jimmy.

The town of Damascus is fourteen miles from the Clark home. Jimmy took the bus back and forth to the school; Helen drove him when he had to stay longer than the bus schedule allowed.

Football hadn't been played at the Damascus school in years. The *Bristol Herald Courier* reported, "Twenty-four inexperienced players, some who have never seen a football game and none of whom has played in competition, have responded to the call of Coach Jim Newton, and daily drills are being held." Jimmy had a schedule of six games for his young, raw team. He chose cocaptains Thomas Martin and Bert Owens to help him mold the players. His manager was student George Ed Barker. The PTA, local businesses and individuals donated funds to help the new team.

Jimmy realized he had a lot of work ahead of him to shape the team for their season. Practices, drills and conditioning lasted for hours after school. The daily rides back and forth from Abingdon to Damascus, especially with all the late practices, were too much to ask of Helen, so many nights, he slept on a cot in the school's basement locker room. Some of the boys would stay there, too. Their coach appeared colorful and a bit glamorous from his war service and travels. Jimmy was charismatic and handsome. The other teachers, administration and staff enjoyed the young man.

His drinking continued—more uninhibited when he was alone in the basement of the school. The boys hung out with him and noticed the bottles of liquor. Soon, a small group of the students regularly drank with their coach. Besides the football players, Jimmy kept company with the other young teachers. He and a fellow male teacher were invited to a female teacher's home for dinner. Miss Tolley still lived with her parents. Her father, W.M. Tolley, later testified that he asked Jimmy to leave shortly after he arrived at the house for dinner. Jimmy hadn't had a drink at their home, but Mr. Tolley said he "smelled intoxicants on him."

JAMES EMMETT NEWTON
Shot fatally in Virginia

Jimmy Newton's Damascus School teacher photograph. *From the* Bristol *(TN)* Herald Courier.

Helen saw Jimmy drifting away from her. His responsibilities at the school occupied his time. Eugene Martin, a football player, testified at the trial that he'd witnessed Jimmy drinking in the basement of the school and that Jimmy had given him whiskey. He also recounted a night when Mrs. Clark (Helen) brought the car to Damascus and Jimmy drove them to the fairgrounds section of Abingdon. Helen sat in the front seat next to Jimmy, and Eugene sat in the back seat. They visited a "bootlegger's place…where whiskey was purchased." He said Mrs. Clark did not pay for the whiskey, nor did she drink any of it. He said they drove around that night, eventually going to Bristol, but Eugene said he did not remember much about the trip or what time they returned home. Jimmy was more than a coach and teacher to the boys; he was their friend, big brother and hero. Most of the boys were just four or five years younger than Jimmy.

Helen inserted herself into Jimmy's daily life, not only driving him to school and football practice but also taking him to Bristol for dinner or on long Sunday drives. Frequently, neighbors saw Helen driving Jimmy and some of the schoolboys around town. At the Abingdon theater, Helen registered for bank night as "Mrs. Jimmy Newton." Word of this circulated around town until Kitty heard it. She mentioned it to Jimmy, but he shrugged it off.

Before the football team's first game, Jimmy presented his plans for a year-round school athletic program to the citizens club of Damascus. On the afternoon of Saturday, September 29, 1945, Damascus High School played their first football game against Meadowview High School. The newspaper reported that "Coach Newton…is well pleased with the condition and spirit of his new squad." The boys played hard. Confusion and frustration dominated the young team. Jimmy, along with the parents, teachers and other students, tried to keep the team's morale up. The result at the end of the afternoon: Meadowview 26, Damascus 0.

That Saturday night, the team huddled in the basement locker room. Jimmy tried to encourage the boys by saying their effort was valiant and that they'd performed well for their opening game. Eventually, after the pep talk, some of the players left to join their girlfriends, while others stayed behind with their coach. Jimmy's hip ached from his pacing along the sideline. He brought out the whiskey.

By late October and early November, the team had gelled. The *Bristol Herald Courier* reported that Coach Newton "will throw a T-formation attack against Virginia tonight—the type of offense that bothered the Orange most this season. The visitors (Damascus), who are returning to football for the first time in five years, have improved steadily this season and expect to play their best ball tonight." The powerhouse of Bristol's Virginia High "Big Orange" beat Damascus 53–0.

When Helen saw the Damascus football team, cheerleaders, band members, faculty and staff boast of Jimmy's accomplishments, she was proud of him and proud of herself for convincing him to stay in Abingdon. He had talked about moving back to Kentucky or even heading to New York City—no doubt encouraged by Andrew Summers. Kitty had left town, which Helen saw as a positive thing in Jimmy's life. That Kitty, Helen thought, is a troublemaker. For the first time in a long time, Helen felt like her old self. She enjoyed going to the football games to watch Jimmy's team. She didn't mind driving Jimmy and some of his players around in her car. If the neighbors gossiped, they were in sore need of entertainment.

America celebrated Armistice Day/Remembrance Day at the request of President Truman on November 11. Jimmy remembered his marine brothers, especially Beet. Depression cloaked him. The household mourned for Hal Jr., whose two-year death anniversary would be on November 21. But before that, Jimmy was found shot on the floor of his bedroom.

10

JIMMY'S LAST DAY

ABINGDON, VIRGINIA
SUNDAY, NOVEMBER 18, 1945

Jimmy's bedroom window faced west. The pale November morning cast little light onto his bed. Half asleep, he tried to heave the lingering nightmares from his head. Beet's face, sweating. Flashes of gunfire from the jungle. Putrid mud. An enemy soldier, eyes to the sky, torso separated from his hips. Jimmy cried.

Footsteps pattered down the hall to the bathroom. Dorothy and Nancy argued about who would go in first. He knew they were preparing for church at Sinking Spring Presbyterian. He had promised to help in the afternoon at St. Thomas Episcopal. The clock showed he had time to make Sunday school if he could clear his thoughts—if he could banish his memories. The hymn "Abide with Me" flickered in the back of his mind. What was he doing with his life? His students brimmed with hope for the future. The war was over. Their young lives would unfurl as they graduated and moved on. His life had shriveled from the war and its physical and emotional damage.

One of his players suggested he go to college with them. Start over? Could he? One fact he knew was that his current situation wasn't working: a job that he wasn't qualified for, a home and family that wasn't his, no one he loved, no one special. Did he deserve love? Does anyone? His Thanksgiving trip to Kentucky would give him time to think and talk with his father. He surveyed his stinging hip, his mental state. Tolerable. Exactly—he could tolerate the day. He decided that he would go to Sunday school. He needed coffee with a bit of bourbon.

He sang in the morning service, which lifted his spirits. At lunch, Dorothy talked of Jack Henderson and their date to the movie that evening. She wanted everyone to go. Jimmy had committed to helping with the afternoon service with Chief Baden, and then he wanted to sleep. The past few weeks, sleep had eluded him. It could have been the practices with the boys or their disappointing losses. He tried to mask his frustration in front of his team, but he could only distract himself with drink, pills or smoke.

⸺⊗⸺

THE AFTERNOON SERVICE DREW several older members of the congregation. The ladies always complimented Jimmy on his singing. Their lavender and rose perfumes conjured thoughts of his mother. He planned to return to his parents on Tuesday.

When he arrived back at the boardinghouse, Nancy and Dorothy prepared chicken and dumplings for supper. As Frances pulled the plates from the china cabinet, Jimmy watched to see if she noticed the pistol tucked in the back. Why it had been placed there, he didn't know. It had mocked him and his weakness from its perch behind the serving platter. He'd taken it in despair late one night when the nightmares wouldn't leave. He'd walked out the back door and sat in the garden among the withered tomato plants and cucumber vines, not belonging there or anywhere. He held the cold, nickel-plated barrel of the gun against his forehead. He thought of Beet, the students in his classroom, the boys on the team, his parents, Helen and the girls. Don't make a mess for them to clean up, he heard the darkness murmur. When he had hardened with resolve and returned to the house, he replaced the gun in the china cabinet. Or did he? He couldn't remember.

After supper, Jimmy went to the front porch for a cigarette. A familiar car drove by, boys hanging out the window. He'd been up and down the mountain roads around Damascus many nights with the boys in that car. Charlie Q. Brown, L.M. Gilpin and Johnny Shoemaker, all part of his football team, turned the car around and parked in front of the house. They called to Jimmy to jump in. L.M. climbed out of the front passenger seat so Jimmy could sit next to Charlie, who drove. The four talked about football and school. Jimmy noticed Helen peeking out her bedroom window at them. "Let's drive," he said. Charlie pulled away from the house just as Johnny fished a bottle of whiskey from under the seat.

They drove over to Mary's Meadows, the old farm of Captain Francis Smith Robertson. The farm spread wide and deep toward the woods that led to the south fork of the Holston River. A secluded, wooded area near the railroad at the edge of Mary's Meadows was a favorite spot for the kids to park. Jimmy and the boys stopped there with their whiskey.

"Must be swell living with four girls," Charlie said. He took a swig of whiskey and handed the bottle to Jimmy. "Mrs. Clark is sweet on you. Hey, Johnny, did you tell Coach about Mrs. Clark coming to the cabin late one night trying to track him down?" The boys had access to a cabin about three miles from Damascus that they used for parties.

"What?" Jimmy asked.

"Yep, you shouldn't have brought her up there, 'cause now if she can't find you, she drives to the cabin to carry you back home." Johnny handed the bottle back to Jimmy. "Like my mother showing up. What if me and a girl were getting together?" The two other boys and Jimmy laughed. Taking offense, Johnny said, "It could happen. You boys are real gassers. The point is, Mrs. Clark has got her thumb on you, Coach. You need to have a chitchat with the lady."

Jimmy grunted and gulped down more whiskey. He thought about Manhattan, nightclubs, sophisticated friends. Maybe at Christmas break, he would visit Andrew and Renato. "Let's go. Dorothy wants to go to the late movie."

Charlie drove them back to the house. They sat in the car talking until Helen marched down the sidewalk to the passenger window, where Jimmy sat.

Helen, frustrated that Jimmy had driven off with the Damascus boys, snapped at him. She demanded he give her the keys to her car and get ready for the movie. "Are you going with us?" she asked.

"After a while," Jimmy said without looking at her.

"After a while will be too late. If you're not going, give me the car keys," she said. He dropped them in her hand. Just like having another child, she thought. One of the boys muttered something, and they laughed. She ignored their juvenility and returned to the house.

Jimmy and the boys followed her inside. The boys settled in the parlor with the Clark girls and Jack. Helen stopped Jimmy in the foyer. She asked if he was going to the movie. When she told him it was a war movie, his head began to ache.

"You go. I can't watch a war," he said.

"Neither can I." Helen looked him straight in the eyes. "You're not the only one injured by the war."

The Damascus boys left because of the coach's expression and Mrs. Clark's tone. Jimmy walked to the car with them to say his goodbyes.

On the porch, Helen called out for her coat. Jimmy ignored her. The girls waited with Jack at the car, ready to leave for Bristol. "Jackass," Helen said to no one in particular. Jimmy waved the boys on and returned to the house. Frances ran back into the house and then came out to say that her mother and Jimmy were not going to the movie. At 8:22 p.m., Jack Henderson, Dorothy, Nancy and Frances left the house in the Clark car for the Cameo Theater in Bristol. They crossed paths with the Damascus boys' car at the intersection of Main and Court Streets. The boys testified that Mrs. Clark and the coach were not with Jack and the girls.

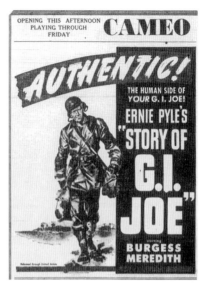

The movie at the Cameo Theater in Bristol, Virginia, on Sunday, November 18, 1945. *From the* Bristol *(TN)* Herald Courier.

WHAT HAPPENED NEXT WAS speculation from the trial witnesses, the prosecution, the defense, neighbors and family. No one was in the room except Helen and Jimmy. Helen never spoke of it.

Jimmy closed the door to his bedroom when he went in. He didn't want to engage with Helen. He'd told her of his decision and that it was not up for debate. He needed quiet. He still wore the sports jacket, white button-down shirt, slacks and Weejuns loafers he'd changed into for dinner. The thought of the war movie and the comments from the boys about Helen's feelings for him caused his head to throb. His hip continually burned and ached. He found the bottle of phenobarbital tablets in the top drawer of the oak chest in the corner. He took the tablets to sleep and then washed them down with paregoric. The paregoric, with its main ingredient of opium, helped soothe his physical pain.

Helen would not take the silent treatment from Jimmy. He was a grown man and, as far as she was concerned, should act like one, which included not icing out people who loved him. Love? She pondered. Did she love him? Her life had improved since Jimmy's arrival that past December. He was her companion. She felt alive again with him, not taking anything away from the love of her life, Hal Clark. Hal had been her complement, the fundamental support of her emotional and physical well-being. Hal's death had broken her. Then to have Little Hal stolen from her by the war—well, she took a deep breath. Jimmy needed her attention. If only someone could have sheltered Hal Jr., he might have made it home. She could protect Jimmy from his troubles. She would not let him go.

Around 8:30 p.m., she went up the stairs. She hesitated at his closed bedroom door. It wasn't latched. She pushed it open.

He seemed startled to see her. Standing next to the chest, he had the borrowed pistol in his hand. He held it out to her. She took it. Jimmy said he had made his decision. He turned away from her as if she didn't matter to him anymore. She yelled, "No! You can't do that!"

Two shots fired. He turned toward her. Two more gunshots blasted. Her ears rang with the sharp burst of the bullets. In the wake of the discharges, the acrid scent of gunpowder settled, and silence shrouded the house.

<hr />

HELEN'S EYES COULDN'T FOCUS. She closed the bedroom door behind her. She reached for the bannister, guiding herself down the stairs. The gun in her right hand had been borrowed from a neighbor. Why did she have it? Her mind didn't connect the pistol to anything, but then her grip on the gun's handle sparked a flashed image. Jimmy had crumpled to the floor.

Get rid of it! The idea flared in her mind. She rushed out the door and down the steps to the sidewalk with the Smith and Wesson .32 in her hand. A look left and right revealed no one around to help her. The Summerses' house sat dark and cold. She rushed behind it and slung the pistol under the back porch.

She wanted to be with her girls. They always took care of things. Back in her house, she picked up the phone to call a taxi. The line was in use by her neighbor. The urgency to move, to do something, prompted her to get her coat and purse. She locked the front door and started walking toward the taxi stand next to the train station. The distance didn't register with her. She couldn't stay in the house and wait for the phone line to call for a cab. She walked.

From her house, Helen walked west, following the sidewalk. Should she go to her brother C.M.? He didn't live far from the Wall Street taxi stand. If only Hal was still here, he would know what to do. Her parents or Hal Jr. could have advised her. She was alone. Step by step, she moved down the sidewalk. Her heels clicked on the bricks, staccato taps. At Pecan Street, she crossed over Plumb Alley to Main Street. A block west, at the Methodist church's corner, she encountered a couple of Dorothy's classmates.

"Young man," she said, trying to catch her breath, "my daughter Dorothy has gone to Bristol and left me behind. Would you drive me to the movie theater?" The boys acted oddly, as if she had caught them out when they should have been home. They hemmed and hawed. Eventually, the little one apologized that he and his friend couldn't help her. She walked on. At the Martha Washington Inn, she hesitated. Should she go back, see about Jimmy? The thought dissipated, and she continued to Wall Street and Steve's Cab Company.

Ernest Wise saw Helen coming to the cab stand. She told him she needed to go to Bristol. Ernest opened the door to the first taxi in the line and placed her in the back seat. He summoned the driver of that cab, Martin G. Mitchell. When Martin got behind the wheel, he greeted Helen and asked for her destination. She told him.

"After we started, she asked me what the fare was, and I told her four dollars," Martin later testified at the trial. "She opened her pocketbook and said she didn't have that much money with her and asked for a blank check. I told her I didn't have one and that she could settle with the cab company the next day. We left Abingdon about 9:00 p.m. and arrived in Bristol about 9:30 p.m. We talked a little, mostly about the weather. She said something about 'Don't tell them I went to Bristol,' but didn't say who she meant by 'them.' I let her out at the theater."

At the Cameo, Helen bought her ticket and found the girls and Jack in the dark theater. She slipped into the row behind them and sat, mind blank, until the end credits rolled and the theater's lights came on.

Nancy saw her mother and asked where Jimmy was. "I don't know," Helen replied, and then she changed the subject.

Gay Leonard explained that she had been told by her mother, Dorothy, that "MeMaw and Uncle C. came to the movie and sat behind the girls." This may have been family legend. The testimony of Nancy in 1946 stated that Helen was alone when she came to the theater. The cab driver's testimony concurred that Helen went to Bristol alone that night.

Jack Henderson drove them back to Abingdon. Arriving at the house at approximately 11:30 p.m., Helen, Nancy and Frances sat in the parlor with Dorothy and Jack. No one noticed any unusual behavior in Helen. She carried her part of the conversation without a hint of anxiety, tension or nervousness. A few minutes later, Helen, Nancy and Frances excused themselves to go to bed. From upstairs, Helen called down to Dorothy to "leave the door unlocked so Jimmy could get in." Helen claimed, later that night, that she had heard a noise at 1:30 or 2:00 a.m. and called to Nancy, who said she thought it was the wind slamming the screen door against the house.

Sleep must have been difficult to achieve for Helen. The house remained quiet. Did she wander the hallways and rooms during the night or go into Jimmy's room? She may have cleaned blood from his rug, although soft tissue wounds sometimes bleed internally and leave little external evidence. She may have arranged his body, since the scene Nancy found in the morning was not characteristic of a suicide or murder.

The next morning, Helen sent her sixteen-year-old daughter to Jimmy's room to find his body.

Nancy knocked on his door, which was open about an inch. Jimmy didn't answer. She pushed the door open and saw Jimmy lying on the floor on his back, arms at his side, legs straight out. He was fully clothed, including his sports jacket and shoes, as if he had gone to sleep on the rug next to his bed. Nancy later said that at first, she thought Jimmy was "drunk or in one of his spells."

"Dorothy," she whispered to her sister, who was coming from the bathroom just a few feet down the hall. "Come here. Jimmy—" Nancy nodded toward the interior of the bedroom. Dorothy peered in. Both girls

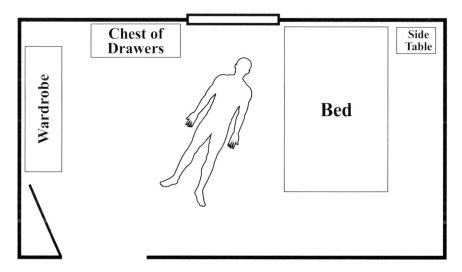

A rendering of Jimmy Newton's body placement when Nancy Clark discovered him in his room. *Author's illustration with body outline image by brgfx on Freepik.*

stood in the doorway staring at Jimmy. "Go in." Nancy pushed Dorothy through the open door.

Face pale, eyes closed, Jimmy looked asleep to Dorothy, but something seemed wrong. "Jimmy," she said. "Wake up." She touched his cheek. Cold. She reached for his wrist in search of a pulse. Nothing.

Dorothy and Nancy rushed down to the parlor. Their mother stood in the doorway to the dining room. "Mother, we think Jimmy is dead," Dorothy said.

"Oh, no," was Helen's response. She sat at the table, both hands flat on its surface and took a deep breath, as if to settle her nerves. "Call your Uncle C."

AT THE ROPP AND Clark Filling Station, C.M. Talbert answered the phone. His niece Dorothy, on the verge of tears and voice cracking, begged him to get to their house. Jimmy was dead. C.M. grabbed Louis Goins, a delivery driver for a local butcher shop who was getting gas for the shop's van, to drive him to the Clark house. Louis Goins later testified that C.M. ran into the house when they arrived. Louis waited outside for about eight minutes before C.M. called him in and had him go upstairs to see the body. He found Jimmy's body stiff. When he came back downstairs, Helen looked at his face and said, "Call Dr. Wolfe."

"Call the doctor?" Louis asked. "I say call the undertaker."

Louis Goins called Paul Campbell, an undertaker for Campbell Funeral Home. Paul was the third outside person to arrive that Monday morning. Paul asked Helen about what happened, and she denied any knowledge. She told him she "heard a noise between 1:30 and 2:00 a.m. but thought it was Jimmy coming home intoxicated and being helped up the stairs by one of the boys." Paul asked Dorothy to call Dr. John Wolfe, the acting coroner. When Dr. Wolfe arrived, he and Paul Campbell went back upstairs to Jimmy's body. Seeing no blood or any indication of foul play, Dr. Wolfe asked if Jimmy had been sick. Dr. Wolfe did not examine the body but asked Paul Campbell to take Jimmy to the funeral home.

At 8:20 a.m. on Monday, November 19, Paul Campbell called Emmett Newton to tell him his son was dead. "He was so shocked that he said only a few words before hanging up, later calling a local undertaker to contact Mr. Campbell," the newspapers reported Emmett Newton's testimony during the trial. "He first learned that his son had been shot when the Associated Press called him shortly before noon that day."

11

THE INVESTIGATION AND ARREST

ABINGDON, VIRGINIA
NOVEMBER 19-NOVEMBER 20, 1945

At the Campbell Funeral Home, Paul Campbell and his staff undressed Jimmy's body. He had been shot multiple times. One bullet fell from his clothing as the staff removed his sport coat, shirt and undershirt. Immediately, they saw two wounds. Two more wounds, presumably exit wounds, were found in Jimmy's back. They called Dr. Wolfe to come to the funeral home. The other bullet, Dr. Wolfe assumed, was in Jimmy's bedroom. Dr. Wolfe called Washington County sheriff J. Trigg Woodward and Commonwealth Attorney Roby C. Thompson. The sheriff and his deputies and Abingdon police chief Frank Cox went to the Clark home looking for another bullet. They did not find it.

Washington County sheriff James Trigg Woodward lived at the county's jail on Park Street in Abingdon. His wife, Martha Alice Lilly, resided there as well, along with their son, Lyle, who acted as the jailor. Twenty to twenty-five inmates, male and female and of all races, were housed at the jail. "When Dr. Wolfe arrived, he immediately called the commonwealth's attorney and me," Sheriff Woodward said.

> The body had been removed to the Paul Campbell Funeral Home before we saw it. At first, it was believed that only two shots had been fired into the body. However, when powder burns were found on the back of the sport coat he was wearing, an X-ray examination was ordered. According to Dr. John A. Wolfe, county coroner, the X-ray disclosed three bullets inside the

body, the fourth having dropped from his clothes. There was one wound in the heart and a second in the shoulder, both fired from the front, a third was under the left shoulder blade about the third or fourth rib and the other was on the left about the ninth rib, according to Dr. Wolfe's unofficial report after examination of the X-ray pictures.

Jimmy had been shot four times at close range—twice in the chest and twice in the back.

At the Clark home, Sheriff Woodward, along with Deputies E.C. Browning, Clarke White, Carl Eskridge and Police Chief Frank Cox, asked Helen about the night before. Helen said that she and Jimmy had planned to go to the Cameo Theater but decided not to because the picture showing was a war movie. After that, she told the sheriff that Jimmy had left the house with two boys from Damascus. She felt "lonesome and decided to go to the show alone, did so and returned with her daughters to the home about 11:30 p.m.," the sheriff described Helen's statement. Helen told them that she heard a noise late in the night, called to Nancy and returned to bed when Nancy said it must have been the wind. The next morning, Nancy discovered Jimmy dead on the floor.

Sheriff J. Trigg Woodward as a deputy, 1928. *Historical Society of Washington County, Virginia.*

During the sheriff's questioning, Helen said she had no pistol but that she did have a rifle and a shotgun. She pondered that Jimmy may have been killed by someone outside the house and carried up the stairs and placed in his room. She stated to the sheriff, his deputies and the police chief that Jimmy had been threatened by "someone in Damascus." The officers searched the house for a pistol but didn't find one.

That Monday afternoon, several of the Damascus football team members and teachers arrived at the Campbell Funeral Home in Abingdon to pay their respects to their mentor and friend. The boys lined up by the open casket with sniffling noses and watery eyes, trying to still their emotions, but as Jimmy's team, they couldn't repress their sorrow. They comforted each other over their shared loss.

Helen did not call the Newtons until about 6:00 p.m. that Monday. Emmett Newton asked if Helen would accompany Jimmy's body to Kentucky. She said she couldn't because one of her girls had the flu. Emmett asked her how Jimmy's death had occurred, and she told him that she didn't know but that someone must have shot Jimmy and carried his body into the house.

That evening, around 9:30 p.m., a deputy knocked on the Clarks' front door to ask Helen to accompany him to Commonwealth Attorney Roby Thompson's office, across from the courthouse. There, Sheriff Woodward informed her of her legal rights. He told her that they had information that she had a pistol that matched the one that killed Jimmy. Helen recalled then that she had borrowed a pistol from W.T. Booker the month before because of rumors of a prowler in the neighborhood. She stated she kept the pistol in her car's glove compartment. The sheriff sent deputies to retrieve it. It wasn't there. She then remembered that she had left it in her china cabinet. The deputies returned to her home to search the china cabinet and the rest of the house, but again, they did not find the gun.

The next morning, Tuesday, November 20, a crowd of Damascus and Abingdon teenagers consisting of high school athletes, cheerleaders, band members and other students joined their parents, clergy members, teachers and community leaders to see Jimmy's body loaded onto train no. 41 bound for Kentucky.

At 1:30 p.m. on Tuesday, Deputy Clarke White escorted Helen to Commonwealth Attorney Roby Thompson's office. On the way, she asked him if a man could shoot himself in the back. Deputy White assured her that wasn't possible.

Bristol Herald Courier reporter Evelyn Hicks, who was staked out in front of the office of the commonwealth's attorney, described Helen going into

Damascus High School students' tearful goodbye to their Coach Jim Newton at the Abingdon train station. *From the* Bristol *(TN)* Herald Courier.

the office. "Mrs. Clark, of slender build, with medium blonde hair and blue eyes, wearing a black high-necked sweater, grey skirt and coat, appeared for questioning at the commonwealth's office in company with Deputy Sheriff Clarke White."

"Mrs. Clark," Sheriff Woodward asked after reviewing all the tales she had told about the night of Jimmy's death and the gun, "with the information you have given us about Sunday night, if you were in my place, who do you think we should charge with the death of James Newton?"

Tears filled her eyes. She glanced down at her folded hands gripping a white handkerchief in her lap. "I guess I would charge myself."

The sheriff told Helen he'd give her another chance to produce the gun and said that Deputy B.K. Barb would accompany her back to her home.

"I volunteered to take her home, and after we entered the car, she started crying," Deputy Barb recounted during the trial. "She said she

Mrs. Hal Clark Charged With Murder In Death Ot Damascus Teacher And Coach James Newtor

DEFENDANT BREAKS UNDER 2 HOURS OF STATE QUESTIONING

Sorrowing Students Mourn Death Of Teacher And Coach

Bullet Ridden Body Left on Floor While Accused Went to Movie Following Ex-Marine's Death

By EVELYN K. HICKS
Staff Correspondent

ABINGDON, Va., Nov. 20.—Mrs. Hal V. Clark, 44-year-old widow, tonight was at liberty under bond of $3,000 following her arrest here at 6 p. m. in the office of Commonwealth's Attorney Roby C. Thompson on a warrant issued on complaint of Mr. Thompson charging that she "killed and murdered James Emmett Newton, III," 22-year-old teacher and high school football coach of Damascus, Va.

The warrant was served by Sheriff J. Trigg Woodward of Washington county who, with his deputies and Abingdon police work-

Sorrowing athletes and cheer leaders of Damascus, Va. high school, pictured at left, were present at Abingdon, Va., yesterday morning when the body of their mentor, James Emmett Newton, 22, was loaded on train 41 over the Norfolk and Western Railway. Newton declined for Anchorage, Ky., his home. Newton was shot to death Sunday night, according to her admission, by Mrs. Hal Clark, of Abingdon, in whose home he resided. The attendants pic-

ture Newton attended Kentucky Military Academy and University of Kentucky before he enlisted in the U. S. Marines at the age of 17. He suffered a shrapnel while fighting the Japanese on Guadalcanal and was discharged from service in 1943. An accompanying story by a staff writer recounts the story of the Abingdon

The headline and frontpage photographs of Damascus students watching Jimmy's coffin being loaded on the train. *From the* Bristol *(TN)* Herald Courier.

was 'trying to shield someone.' She then told me that Newton had shot himself but that she didn't want to tell that he had committed suicide." By this time, the deputy had driven her the short distance to her house. She asked Deputy Barb if a man could shoot himself twice in the chest. He told her that was entirely possible. Helen asked him to go back for the sheriff and Roby Thompson so she could show them where the gun was. "When I drove back in front of the office," Deputy Barb continued, "I could see Sheriff Woodward through the window and called to him and the commonwealth's attorney to come down."

The sheriff and Roby Thompson left Thompson's office and climbed into the back seat of the patrol car. The sheriff stated, "Mrs. Clark said she had been protecting someone and that 'the someone was Jimmy's father.' She had wanted to tell what happened, but Jimmy had told her if anything happened to him, his father would die because he had a bad heart."

At the Clark home, Helen led them next door to the back lawn of L.P. Summers's home. She pointed to the place where she had thrown the small gun under the porch. Deputy Barb crawled under the porch about four feet and returned with a Smith and Wesson .32-caliber pistol. The gun contained five empty cartridges.

They returned to the Clark house. Helen led them upstairs. In the small bedroom where Jimmy had died, Helen told the men her account of what happened. After she and Jimmy decided not to attend the movie in Bristol, he went to his room. A short time later, she went to the room and found him in front of the chest of drawers, "getting the gun out and pointing it toward himself." She said she screamed, "You can't do that!" And Jimmy replied, "Why can't I?" Then he shot himself twice. She knocked the gun out of his hand. It fell on the bed. She grabbed for the gun. Jimmy began to fall. As she tried to support Jimmy and hold the gun, the pistol discharged "two or three times." She asked if Jimmy wanted her to call a doctor. She said that he replied, "No, I'm dying." With that answer, she went down the stairs, threw the pistol under the Summerses' porch, locked her front door and took a taxi to join her daughters at the movie. When she returned with the girls, they all went to bed, and next the morning, she asked her daughter to call Jimmy. Nancy immediately ran back downstairs to tell her about finding the body.

Helen gave a statement to Sheriff Woodward and Roby Thompson, as reported by the *Lebanon News*:

MRS. ELLEN T. CLARK

Ellen "Helen" Talbert Clark outside the courthouse. *From the* Bristol *(TN)* Herald Courier.

I was very much attached to James. So were my daughters, Dorothy, eighteen years old; Nancy, sixteen and my youngest, ten years old.

He roomed with us. His conduct was always excellent. He was a gentleman.

On the day of the tragedy my daughters went to a movie at Bristol. Everything was quiet about the house.

I did not hear Mr. Newton stirring about in his room and went there to see if everything was all right.

I opened the door gently; believing he might be asleep. What I saw astounded me. He was standing near a dresser with a pistol in his hand. I rushed in and tried to seize the weapon. He struggled with me, saying he was going to kill himself. Then he fired into his chest. I kept struggling. I was terribly excited.

While I was trying to wrest the gun from his hand it was discharged twice and the bullets entered his back. He crumpled up and fell on the floor.

I was so bewildered I didn't know what to do. I seemed to be in a trance.

I took the pistol next door and placed it under a neighbor's porch. I did not dare say a word.

All I could think of was my daughters. So I went to a movie and joined them.

James was so fine, so straightforward and popular with everyone. My story may seem strange, but it is the truth, so help me.

Outside the office, reporter Evelyn Hicks changed her description of Helen for the newspaper account: "Mrs. Clark, pale, haggard and visibly under tension told her story in the commonwealth attorney's office in the presence of Sheriff Woodward, Mr. Thompson, Deputies Sheriff B.K. Barb, B. Clarke White and E.C. Browning."

Thirty-six hours after the discovery of Jimmy's body, Sheriff Woodward charged Helen with the murder of Jimmy Newton. Her brothers C.M. and Willie posted her $3,000 bond to take her home.

12

THE COMMUNITY WHISPERS

ABINGDON, VIRGINIA
NOVEMBER 21, 1945–MAY 5, 1946

News of the murder of Jimmy Newton was picked up by the Associated Press. Newspapers from across the country published the story. The sensation of a forty-four-year-old, lonely widow murdering a twenty-two-year-old World War II veteran and high school coach intrigued readers. The newspaper stories hinted at sex, jealously and a woman scorned.

Reporters used words such as *death house, slayer, bullet-riddled, comely widow, bizarre* and *weird* to stir interest and readership.

Helen's brothers C.M. and Willie hired the best attorneys they could find. George M. Warren was a member of Virginia's general assembly and "one of the best-known criminal lawyers in Southwest Virginia." Embree W. Potts, a former Abingdon mayor, also joined the defense team. Embree Potts had worked with Hal Clark in leading the town's sewer project six years earlier. George Warren requested to meet with Helen, but she had C.M. tell the attorney she was too ill to have a visitor.

On Thursday, November 22, Thanksgiving Day, Helen called the Newton home in Anchorage, Kentucky, between 3:00 and 4:00 p.m. to inform Emmett that she had been charged with murder. She also requested that Emmett come to Abingdon as soon as possible. Emmett and his brother-in-law, Gil Cowherd, arrived at the Clark home around 3:00 p.m. that Monday, November 26. Helen told them about Jimmy's death—the version she'd told Sheriff Woodward. Emmett asked to see Jimmy's room. Helen led them upstairs and related the tale of seeing Jimmy pull a gun from a drawer of the chest and fire at himself. Then recounted the struggle for the gun and it discharging several times. Jimmy's uncle Gil did most of the talking to Helen. The only thing Emmett was able to ask was, "Why didn't you call a doctor for my son?" She turned to him, hesitated and said, "You know he didn't like doctors."

That same day, the Washington County Court grand jury convened, and Vista Ellen Talbert Clark was indicted for murder. Judge Walter H. Robertson set December 18 for the trial's starting date.

Helen went under the care of Dr. George A. Wright, the former superintendent of Southwestern Virginia State Hospital (formerly the Southwestern Lunatic Asylum) for psychiatric observation and a complete examination while she was a patient at Lee Memorial Hospital in Marion until December 15.

George Warren and Embree Potts told the court that Helen's mental condition "was such at present that her life would be endangered by a trial at this time," stated the *Richmond Times Dispatch*. Dr. George Wright explained that her condition had improved, but she had been "highly nervous" and "a very sick woman" when she entered his care. George Warren seemed to set the groundwork for Helen's defense.

The community may have thought a lot of different things about Helen Clark and her indictment, but she was Hal Clark's widow. With that came a measure of respect. The trial hadn't started, so no one had heard the full story.

Jimmy's friends and associates couldn't imagine that the charismatic young man had died by suicide. That type of thing didn't happen in good families, certainly not to a war veteran who had so honorably served.

"People are good at putting on the show, pushing it to the background, and only when there are certain triggers does it boil to the top," Army Major General Rodney D. Fogg (retired) explained about PTSD. "Triggers could be a time of year." Jimmy had traumatic events occur in October, November and early December. Jimmy had been injured in Guadalcanal in October. Clarke Beetlestone had gone MIA in November. Pearl Harbor occurred on December 7. Helen's traumatic anniversaries included Hal's death in October and Hal Jr.'s death in November. "When that time frame rolled around, in the back of his head, and when he went to sleep, the nightmares would start. He wouldn't have had them all the time, but he would have them during that time. They're triggered because of the trauma that happened in the autumn of the year." People around Jimmy would have known he wasn't himself, or at least the persona he presented

Parks-Belk Department Store on Main Street. *Historical Society of Washington County, Virginia.*

the rest of the year. "The image of a soldier wasn't someone who would need help. Suicide is a big problem in the military to this day," Major General Fogg added.

The other teachers and staff at the Damascus school may have noticed Jimmy spending more nights in the basement locker room. Some may have ignored this change in his behavior because of the football team's struggle to score in their games. There were times the handsome, young marine laughed and sang. The students adored him, especially his football team members. The thought of him dying by suicide would never be believed with his community in Damascus.

In Abingdon, Helen's neighbors and friends may have drifted from their social interactions with her after Hal died, but the ladies of Valley Street buzzed with the latest sightings of Helen Clark with the young coach. He seemed much more like a teenager than an adult, especially while he was running around with the high school boys. The talk about town was that he made a good match for young Dorothy. She was beautiful. Remember, they said, that Dorothy won the Kiwanis club's beauty pageant and was crowned Miss Washington County of 1944 at the Zephyr Theatre. He may have been a little old for her, but the young man had served in Guadalcanal.

At the Parks-Belk store's balcony, a trio of women who were shopping spotted Helen Clark and little Frances on the main sales floor. "How I wish

Helen hadn't lost Hal," one woman remarked. "Seems like since his death, then her mother and father's deaths, she has just…gone off the deep end." The other two ladies *tsk-tsked* and shook their heads. "Now, she's going to be judged by a bunch of county farmers for shooting that boy." The ringleader of the conversation continued after she checked to be sure she wouldn't be overheard by any other customers or sales girls, "I can't blame her for running around with him, but you keep that private and you certainly don't go off your rocker and shoot your lover." Other similar conversations spread across the town in parlors, hair salons, stores and at the clotheslines in backyards. Helen and her daughters became the subjects of chatting women, men, teenagers and children.

The Washington County Circuit Court convened on Monday, January 28. Helen's case was on the docket. The case received another continuance. The March 25 circuit court issued an additional continuance, because Deputy Sheriff E.C. Browning, a crucial witness for the prosecution, was in Johnston Hospital for an appendicitis operation. Another continuance was issued the next month due to the illness of defense attorney George Warren.

The trial was set for May 6, with Judge Walter H. Robertson presiding.

Circuit Court of Washington County, Virginia, 1934. Group photograph with the judges, attorneys and sheriff. *Historical Society of Washington County, Virginia.*

George Warren enhanced his defense team. Along with former Abingdon mayor Embree Potts, Mr. Warren added fellow Bristol attorney Emory Widener and Abingdon attorney Tom Hutton.

The prosecution team consisted of Commonwealth Attorney Roby C. Thompson and Fred C. Parks of Abingdon, who had been hired by the Newton family to assist.

Washington County and Abingdon, the county seat, were close-knit communities, especially in the town leadership, legal and law enforcement brotherhoods. Fred Parks (prosecution), Roby Thompson (prosecution), George Warren (defense) and Tom Hutton (defense) had all served as honorary pallbearers at Hal Clark's funeral just three years before. They had known Helen and Hal for years. Their children went to school and church and played on sports teams with the Clark children. These men had, themselves, grown up with Hal Clark and Helen Talbert Clark. No matter what their past interactions and memories were of Helen, they had to rely on the facts of the case as they would discover them and present them to the jury for the benefit of their clients.

13

THE TRIAL

ABINGDON, VIRGINIA
MAY 6–MAY 13, 1946

The town buzzed with interest and excitement at hearing the potential sordid details of the relationship between Jimmy Newton and Helen Clark. Jimmy's parents, Emmett and Edythe; his sister, Mabel; and his uncle Gil arrived for the trial and lodged at the Martha Washington Inn.

Twenty-four men were summoned for a jury pool, or venire, before the trial, and then circuit court clerk Charles Booth called another twenty-four prospective jurors in case the first twenty-four didn't yield a jury to satisfy the attorneys.

MONDAY, MAY 6, 1946

Observers filled the courtroom, hallway and stairs to watch the murder trial of Helen Clark. The first day was a disappointment to the spectators. When the court convened at 9:00 a.m., Emory Widener, defense counsel, had issue with the process of the selection of the venire. Judge Walter H. Robertson called the attorneys for the commonwealth and the defense, along with Helen, into his chambers. The defense "contended that some of the venire's names had been picked from the box by the jury commissioner and some by the court, and that all should be picked by the court." After a three-hour discussion, Judge Robertson quashed the venire, or rejected the jury pool. In an early afternoon action, the judge ordered a new venire summoned and set to reconvene the next morning at 9:00 a.m.

With the court adjourned, the Newtons agreed to be interviewed by *Bristol Herald Courier* reporter Evelyn Hicks. In the Newtons' hotel room, Ms. Hicks asked about Jimmy's background. "Jimmy was always such an affectionate boy and was kind to everyone, especially to old ladies," Edythe told the reporter in a poke at Helen, although Edythe was seventeen years older than Helen. The reporter portrayed Edythe as "a refined, motherly woman with gray hair and saddened blue eyes." Emmett was described as "a kind-faced man." Jimmy's sister, Mabel, was described as "a pretty dark-haired woman." Edythe showed the reporter a newspaper clipping from New Smyrna on Jimmy's death that detailed the work he did with the Sea Scouts and his musical contributions to the community. She told of her son's education, him joining the Marines Corps after the attack on Pearl Harbor, his service in the Pacific and his injury at Guadalcanal. She explained how Jimmy became stranded by the snowstorm in Abingdon on his way to see Clarke Beetlestone's parents. Mrs. Hicks tried to get the family to discuss the trial, but they declined to comment.

TUESDAY, MAY 7, 1946

At the 9:00 a.m. opening of the court, circuit court clerk Charles Booth read the indictment against Vista Ellen Talbert Clark. Helen "spoke firmly and appeared composed as she pled innocent." With the juror selection process underway, fewer spectators showed up in the morning session.

The court proceeded with twenty-six potential jurors. Clerk Booth asked "if they had any scruples against inflecting the death penalty," signaling that the state was considering capital punishment for a guilty verdict. By 11:30 a.m., thirteen men had been accepted from the morning's pool of twenty-six. The other potential jurors were excused due to their strong opinions of the case. Court officers rushed to summon another twenty-six men for questioning to complete a venire that would be trimmed to twelve members for the trial. Judge Robertson recessed court until 3:00 p.m. for more juror questioning. The courtroom filled with spectators in the afternoon. Officers were not able to summon all the names drawn and deliver them to court in time. Judge Robertson adjourned the court at 3:15 p.m.

Above: Two of the participants in the trial: Fred Parks (*second from left*) and Judge Walter H. Robertson (*fifth from left*). *Historical Society of Washington County, Virginia.*

Right: An early twentieth-century postcard of the Washington County, Virginia Court House in Abingdon, Virginia. *Author's collection.*

115

WEDNESDAY, MAY 8, 1946

Juror selection was completed in the morning, with a jury of eleven farmers and one merchant selected: Claude G. Clifton, Ira T. Crabtree, Howard Aven, C.T. Wilkinson, Claude Garrett, Robert Bott, W.T. Dye, Luther Dutton, H.B. Gray, C.E. Minnich, W.P. McCray (all farmers) and L.R. Brown (a merchant).

Commonwealth Attorney Roby Thompson promised the jury that the prosecution would prove Helen killed Jimmy in a "frenzy of jealousy." In his opening statement, he asserted, "Mrs. Clark was desperately in love with Newton, and she resented his attention to other girls." He added that on the night of November 18, Helen and Jimmy had "quarreled on the porch of her home as her daughters and their boyfriend left for a show." He added that within fifteen minutes, she had killed Jimmy, hidden the gun and walked away from the house. "This is one of those tragedies of a jealous woman who would rather kill her suitor than lose him to someone else. It is your duty to impose such punishment as the seriousness of the crime justifies."

Defense attorney Tom Hutton stated to the jury that the indictment meant little and that the jury should make their decision by considering the law and the evidence presented. He then began with a description of Helen: "Mrs. Clark is a lifelong resident of Abingdon. She is the widow of Hal Clark. A finer citizen never lived in Abingdon. He was a member of the town council and a businessman here. Her son was killed in action after volunteering at the age of eighteen. There was a void in this mother's heart who had lost her father and mother as well as her husband and son." He said that Jimmy had killed himself. Helen was so horrified by seeing his death by suicide that she was in shock when she hid the pistol and left the house without notifying anyone. He claimed Helen was not in love with Jimmy, but she showed him the same kindness and affection that she showed other young men "to fill the void in her life created by the death of her son, Hal Clark Jr., who was killed in action in World War II." He continued outlining the defense's position that Jimmy had sustained injuries in an automobile wreck as a young boy and suffered from his war wounds. Hutton added Jimmy had repeatedly stated to friends that he had not long to live and would rather "end it all" with his own hand than die in pain and had tried to kill himself before by taking an overdose of drugs.

The prosecution called Dr. John Wolfe, the coroner. He said that Jimmy's death could have been caused either by one of the bullets that entered his body from the front or the bullets that entered from the back. More than one fatal shot had been fired.

Gil Cowherd, Jimmy's uncle, took the stand. He answered questions about Jimmy's life before he arrived in Abingdon. He also answered questions about his trip with Emmett Newton to the Clark boardinghouse the week after Jimmy's death. Gil described Helen's explanation of the night. "When I asked her why she had hidden the gun and had not called a doctor or notified police, she couldn't answer. She said, 'I wish to God I had.' She declared that if she had done so, she realized she wouldn't have been charged with murder." Gil looked straight at Helen. She sat at the table with her attorneys, staring at her hands folded in her lap.

Paul Campbell from the Campbell Funeral Home explained that Louis Goins had called him to come to the Clark home. Mr. Goins had driven C.M. Talbert to Mrs. Clark's house, and he (Paul Campbell) arrived before the coroner. He saw Jimmy upstairs and then returned downstairs without moving the body. He went back upstairs when Dr. Wolfe arrived. The doctor did not examine the body on site but asked Mr. Campbell to take Jimmy's body to the funeral home for an autopsy. There was no blood and no evidence of foul play. The defense had no questions for Paul Campbell.

Louis Goins testified that he'd been at the filling station with his delivery truck when C.M. Talbert received a phone call from one of the Clark girls and asked him to drive him to Mrs. Clark's house. When they arrived, C.M. jumped out of the truck and ran inside. Mr. Goins stayed by the truck on the street. About eight minutes later, C.M. Talbert came to the front door and called for Mr. Goins to come in. The Clarks sent him upstairs to see the body. He touched Jimmy's arm. It was cold and stiff. He reported to Helen and C.M. what he found. "Mrs. Clark told him to call Dr. Wolfe," reporter Evelyn Hicks wrote. "The court rapped for order when the capacity crowd of spectators laughed as he said he replied, 'Call the undertaker.'" The defense didn't question Louis Goins.

Jack Henderson took the stand. He said he arrived at the Clark home that Sunday and talked with Jimmy and the three Damascus boys sitting in their car. He said Helen asked for her coat and that the "misunderstanding" between Helen and Jimmy ended with her calling him "jackass." In Bristol, Jack said, Mrs. Clark came into the theater about half an hour after he and the girls arrived. "She said she was lonesome at home, got scared and came to the show. We arrived at their home about 11:30 p.m., went in and sat down, talked for a while, and then I went home, as it was getting late."

Commonwealth Attorney Roby Thompson asked Jack if Jimmy had ever talked of suicide. Jack said Jimmy had told him that, once, his father had taken a gun from him because he'd threatened to kill himself. Then Mr.

Thompson asked if Jimmy "went with Dorothy" to dispel the rumors of a relationship. Jack answered, "No. If he went, the whole family went." Roby Thompson walked away from the witness stand, stood at the prosecution table and sighed. He turned back to Jack and set his feet apart. "Did you, on account of the relationship between Jimmy and Mrs. Clark, threaten to kill him?"

The defense attorneys jumped to their feet, objected and insisted on a mistrial. The mistrial was overruled, but their objection was sustained.

Roby Thompson and Fred Parks called each of the Damascus boys: Charles Q. Brown Jr., sixteen; L.M. Gilpin Jr., seventeen; and Johnny Shoemaker, sixteen. Each told a similar account of that Sunday afternoon. Roby Thompson asked Charlie if he saw Jimmy and Mrs. Clark together frequently. Usually,

NOMINATED FOR FEDERAL JUDGESHIP
Roby Thompson, Abingdon lawyer, was selected yesterday to be federal judge for Western Virginia. The nomination is subject to Senate approval.

Commonwealth's attorney Roby Thompson. *From the* Bristol *(TN)* Herald Courier.

they were together at football games, Charlie said, and the girls were with Mrs. Clark. She sometimes drove Jimmy to the school, Charlie added.

L.M. added that Mrs. Clark had come looking for Jimmy at their party cabin one night. Thompson asked if the girls had been with Mrs. Clark on that occasion, and L.M. said he had seen only Mrs. Clark.

All three of the boys stated there was "no actual quarrel" that evening between Mrs. Clark and Jimmy. "She could have asked for the keys in a nicer manner," Charlie said. Johnny stated that "Mrs. Clark seemed a little upset."

Billy Vance, a seventeen-year-old Abingdon student, said he met an out-of-breath Mrs. Clark on the sidewalk by the Methodist church as he turned the corner the night of the murder.

Ernest Wise and Martin Mitchell, drivers for Steve's Cabs, described Helen's mission to get to Bristol.

At 4:45 p.m. on Wednesday, Judge Robertson adjourned the court. Roby Thompson and Fred Parks had not proven a quarrel or a jealous motive, wrote Evelyn Hicks.

THURSDAY, MAY 9, 1946

Sheriff J. Trigg Woodward took the stand to recount the statements made by Helen during the thirty-six-hour period between the time Jimmy's body was found that Monday morning and Helen's arrest around 6:30 p.m. the following day, Tuesday, November 20, 1945. The sheriff had warned Helen that there would possibly be a trial and that anything she stated might be used against her. He recounted the number of times they searched for the murder weapon and Helen's multiple musings on its location, concluding with Helen leading them to L.P. Summers's home. Deputy Barb retrieved the pistol from under the back porch. The gun was a .32-caliber Smith and Wesson "squeezer."

The defense council clashed with the introduction of Helen's sworn statement from the time of her arrest. It related the same story the sheriff told the court. The statement was read into the record. The statement included Helen saying that she'd made up her mind in the taxi ride to Bristol to not tell anyone what had happened to Jimmy and that she believed that Jimmy was dead by the time she went down the stairs.

Next on the stand, Deputy Clarke White corroborated the sheriff's statements. He added that when he picked up Mrs. Clark at 1:30 p.m. that Tuesday, she asked if it was possible for Jimmy to have shot himself in the back. Deputy White said he told her no, it wasn't possible.

Commonwealth Attorney Roby Thompson strove to prove Jimmy had not died by suicide with his questioning of Deputy E.C. Browning. Deputy Browning stated he'd received weekly firearms instruction for over two years from Radford Ordnance Works. He testified that the pistol, a .32-caliber Smith and Wesson "squeezer," could not have discharged automatically into Jimmy's back as Mrs. Clark tried to keep him from falling. The gun had a spring safety handle that had to be squeezed at the same time the trigger was pulled.

Roby Thompson's partner in the prosecution, Attorney Fred Parks, asked Deputy Browning to estimate how close the gun had to have been held to Jimmy to produce the powder stains on his coat. The defense team shouted their objections. Judge Robertson allowed the deputy to show the court. Reporter Evelyn Hicks wrote, "He estimated that the one fired from the front, which went through the right edge of the jacket, had been fired from a distance of from thirteen to fifteen inches; the one into the left shoulder about the same; the one in the back nearest the center with the gun held against the coat with some pressure; and the other one in the back about fifteen to eighteen inches."

Fred Parks requested Deputy Browning put on Jimmy's sports jacket and demonstrate whether the gun could have been fired from those distances if Jimmy had been holding the pistol. Judge Robertson sustained vigorous defense objections to the demonstration.

A 1943 advertisement with the Smith and Wesson .32 "squeezer" safety pistol (*lower left*). *Author's collection.*

Deputy B.K. Barb echoed the statements of the sheriff and the other two deputies. He described his and Helen's interactions on their drive back to her home after her questioning. She had asked if someone could shoot themselves twice. Deputy Barb replied that it was "possible with a small gun, but not in the back."

Paul Campbell explained that he and his son, Sam Campbell, had undressed Jimmy's body and found a bullet, which dropped from the clothes.

This was the first indication that Jimmy had met a violent death. The bullet was entered as an exhibit.

The prosecution team introduced a sport coat bearing four bullet holes and gunpowder burns along with a white shirt and an undershirt, both showing brown-red bloodstains around the four entry points of the bullets on their bright white cotton fabric. Undertaker Sam Campbell identified the items as the clothing he had removed from Jimmy's body on the morning of November 19.

Mrs. E.F. Barker, the mother of George Ed Barker, a student from Damascus high school, stated she had stopped at the Clark home on Monday morning after learning of Jimmy's death. Mrs. Clark told her that Jimmy had been shot. Mrs. Barker quoted Helen, explaining that a "man at Damascus" (whom she named) might have shot him. Mrs. Barker said Mrs. Clark told her the Damascus man had threatened Jimmy's life.

FRIDAY, MAY 10, 1946

The Friday morning testimony focused on James Emmett Newton Sr., Jimmy's father. Emmett recounted Jimmy's education, his talent as a musician and his military service. Defense attorney Tom Hutton insinuated that Jimmy had once gone AWOL (absent without leave), so Roby Thompson posed the allegation to Emmett. "Mr. Newton made an emphatic denial that his son had ever been guilty of a breach of service and introduced his honorable discharge, which described his conduct as good," reported the evening newspaper in Bristol. When Roby Thompson asked if Jimmy had ever threatened suicide, Emmett replied, "Absolutely not." Helen had sworn Jimmy had in her signed statement she made at the time of her arrest. The sworn and signed statement had been read to the court the day before. Emmett added he had never asked Mrs. Clark if his son's death was the result of suicide. Jimmy had a "nervous condition" after returning from the Pacific because of his war injuries, he said.

In cross-examination from the defense attorneys, Emmett said he did not object to his son working for Mrs. Clark and that the relationship between the two families was pleasant. He claimed that his son had said Mrs. Clark "treated him like a mother." He said he "had never dreamed of Mrs. Clark being in love" with his son "until after the shooting."

Commonwealth Attorney Roby Tompson concluded the prosecution's case, but the premise of Helen's "frenzy of jealousy over attention to other girls" was not proven. But motive isn't required for a conviction. The prosecution did not establish a clear murder motive, but Emmett's denial that Jimmy had ever attempted suicide was "a blow to the defense." The main fact the jury would remember was that the .32-caliber Smith and Wesson pistol was a "squeezer" and incapable of discharging by accident.

The court reconvened in the afternoon, and the defense attorneys called character witnesses to vouch for Helen's "reputation as a moral, upright woman," the Bristol newspaper described. Then Nancy Clark took the stand to defend her mother. She "emphatically denied that the relationship between her mother and their young boarder had been anything other than that between a mother and her son." Attorney Fred Parks for the commonwealth cross-examined Nancy. "Her testimony remained unshaken throughout grilling," Evelyn Hicks wrote in the newspaper.

Nancy introduced a suicide note that she claimed Jimmy had written while in Florida and given to her to deliver to his father. She said that two hours after he gave her the note, Jimmy took about one-third of a bottle of one hundred phenobarbital tablets. The note was on Nancy's school notebook paper that she said she had given him while she was doing her homework. The note, placed into exhibit, read: "Dear Dad: You know my actions better than anyone else so whatever happens, I'll be happy. Mrs. Clark and her family have been wonderful to me. Remember this. Love you J.E." Nancy said Jimmy refused to allow them to summon a doctor after he took the tablets but had them call an Episcopal minister. "The minister, a sailor, another man and her mother had worked over Jimmy most of the night," the newspaper reported. The prosecution didn't question why half of Jimmy's suicide note was devoted to clearing the Clark family's responsibility for his death.

Nancy added, "Jimmy said mother was the only mother he ever had, and our home was his only home." Edythe and Emmett Newton, along with Jimmy's sister, Mabel, and uncle Gil were in the courtroom to hear this. Nancy quoted Jimmy as telling her, "He disliked his own mother very much and said that they quarreled whenever they were together for very long."

Fred Parks asked Nancy when she first noticed her mother had arrived at the Cameo Theater that evening. "After the movie was over," Nancy said. She said she asked her mother where Jimmy was and that Helen replied she didn't know. Nancy described the family returning together after the show. She said she didn't sleep well. "She said there was nothing to arouse her suspicion that there was a dead man in the house and told of her mother's calling to her later to ask if she had heard a noise. She didn't know whether her mother slept well that night," the newspaper reported of the trial testimony.

The defense, led by George Warren, called Kitty Smyth to the stand. Her navy fitted jacket with a matching skirt accentuated her natural curves. Kitty wore her dark hair in a Lauren Becall wave to her padded shoulders. The attorneys and jury seemed to sit taller as she took the witness chair. Kitty said she first met Jimmy in Oak Ridge and said they corresponded. She explained that she had boarded at the Clark home while she attended Virginia Intermont College in Bristol and that by the time Jimmy stopped by the Clark home in December 1944, she'd moved to another boardinghouse. She and Jimmy had a small argument, since she hadn't expected a visit and had made other plans. She swore that Mrs. Clark treated Jimmy like a son and that the daughters treated him like a brother.

"Didn't you tell Deputies Sheriff Barb and Browning Mrs. Clark had registered for bank night at an Abingdon theater as Mrs. Jimmy Newton?" Kitty was asked. She responded that she had heard the rumor. She didn't think anything of it. They were not dating but were friends. She stated she'd been out of town lately, visiting Cuba and Charleston, South Carolina, and attending school in Rochester, New York.

The defense's other witnesses included John Hortenstine, who had gone hunting with Jimmy on November 16, two days before his death. John claimed that Jimmy drank "most of a fifth of liquor" during their hunting trip. Later that same day, he spotted Jimmy at Emory and Henry College attending a basketball tournament, where Jimmy consumed another fifth. "He declared Jimmy had told him the Clark home was the only home he ever had, and that Mrs. Clark treated Jimmy as a son" the newspaper reported. Gay Leonard mentioned John Hortenstine before knowing he had testified in her grandmother's trial. "All these guys were crazy about mother [Dorothy]," Gay said. "One was Johnny Hortenstine, who was in London during the war and sent mother a pair of English riding boots." Dorothy treasured the riding boots and kept them all her life. John Hortenstine's testimony may have been shaded by his feelings for Dorothy and the Clark family.

School janitor T.C. Minton confirmed that Jimmy sometimes spent the night in the basement of the high school at Damascus, where he had a cot in the locker room. He said that he had seen Jimmy intoxicated; although, under cross-examination, Mr. Minton admitted he'd never actually seen Jimmy take a drink.

Principal S.W. Edmondson stated Jimmy had told him about his injury in Guadalcanal and that the "young coach appeared to be highly nervous."

JOHN HORTENSTINE

Hi-Y Club; Football; Basketball.

John Hortenstine, Jimmy's hunting buddy and an admirer of Dorothy Clark. *William King High School's* The Scroll *yearbook, 1939.*

On cross-examination, Principal Edmondson described Jimmy as "highly popular with the student body and that the whole football team sometimes followed Newton when he went to lunch. He was the most talented and popular man I ever saw," Principal Edmondson stated. "He did more things well than any young man I knew."

During the trial, newspaper reporter Evelyn Hines watched Helen.

> *Mrs. Clark, Gold Star mother, sat through the fifth day of the trial with outward composure. Throughout the lengthy testimony of the numerous witnesses who have gone before the jury to tell their stories of different phases of the tragedy, Mrs. Clark has maintained a calm demeanor. Appearing daily in the courtroom dressed in a long black coat, black dress and small black hat with a veil on the back, only her gloved hands toying nervously in her lap with her purse or a fountain pen have indicated her state of perturbation.*

SATURDAY, MAY 11, 1946

Dr. George Wright, head of Lee Memorial Hospital in Marion, Virginia, took the stand and swore that he didn't believe Mrs. Clark was responsible for her actions and statements following the death of Jimmy Newton. His findings from her hospitalization between November 28 and December 15, 1945, concluded she was in "a neurotic and anemic condition, culminating an operation for toxic goiter fifteen years ago and aggravated by the fact that she is passing through the climacteric (change of life) plus the loss of her husband, son, father and mother all within the last five years."

The jury box of middle-aged and elderly men shifted in their seats awkwardly with the mention of menopause.

"We do not know why she did the things she did, such as hiding the pistol, taking a cab for Bristol and telling no one," Dr. Wright said.

Under cross-examination from the commonwealth, Dr. Wright acknowledged he hadn't seen Helen as a patient before. When she was admitted to his care on November 28, 1945, she was in a highly nervous state and had already been charged with the murder. Roby Thompson asked whether dwelling on thoughts of a murder charge might make anyone nervous, and Dr. Wright replied, "It certainly would." Dr. Wright was the final defense witness.

The defense did not call Helen to the stand to testify on her own behalf and rested its case shortly before noon.

Jimmy's father, Emmett, was recalled by Fred Parks to examine the Florida suicide note that Nancy had introduced the day before. Mr. Newton asserted the note was not in his son's handwriting.

By 1:30 p.m., both the defense and commonwealth concluded their cases. The jury was sequestered for the remainder of the weekend. "The jurors lolled in their hotel rooms, reading newspapers, from which accounts of the trial had been eliminated, and sedately ate their meals," reported the newspaper.

SUNDAY, MAY 12, 1946

Monday morning's edition of the Bristol newspaper reported what had been discussed on Sunday and what spectators in the court could expect: "Instructions to the jury may require possibly two hours, a part of which will be consumed in the court's chambers while attorneys argue such items as: 'reasonable doubt'; that the failure of the defendant to take the witness stand shall not be held against her; points involving Mrs. Clark's failure to report the death of Newton immediately after it occurred."

MONDAY, MAY 13, 1946

Crowds filed into the courthouse, jockeying for a seat, "filling every inch of the courtroom, the hall and lining the stairway outside," reported Evelyn Hicks for the *Bristol Herald Courier*. The morning was consumed by the attorneys consulting with Judge Robertson in the judge's chambers on instructions for the jury. Court recessed at 1:10 p.m. Many of the spectators unwrapped the lunches they had packed and ate at their seats or while standing outside the courtroom, not wanting to lose their coveted spots. When the court reconvened at 2:30 p.m., Judge Robertson read the instructions to the jury, which included the six possible verdicts: innocent, murder in the first degree, murder in the second degree, voluntary manslaughter, involuntary manslaughter or assault.

Helen wore a black dress, as she had throughout the trial, no makeup and sat between her brother C.M. and daughter Dorothy. Nancy sat next to her sister. Little Frances continued to stay with her aunts and uncles. The only movement the spectators saw was Helen twisting a white lace handkerchief as she listened to the jury's instructions and possible verdicts for her future. She wrapped the handkerchief around both hands so tightly that Dorothy reached over to pull it loose from her fists when Fred Parks walked to the front of the courtroom.

Attorney Parks paced before the jury box and repeated the state's position that the widowed Clark was "madly in love" with young Jimmy and had shot him in a jealous rage because of his affections for other girls. "When you have found her guilty, as under the law and evidence, you must do, I am sorry to say, you will judge her in fixing punishment. Others might be motivated by the same passions and illicit desires. You have not merely to punish her but to maintain the majesty of the law. Life must be protected. I leave to you whatever punishment you see fit to impose, whether first- or second-degree murder."

The suicide note introduced into evidence by Nancy, said to have been written by Jimmy in Florida, was fraudulent, Mr. Parks stressed. Mr. James Emmett Newton Sr. had sworn on the stand that the handwriting was not his son's. Fred Parks told the jury the handwriting was that of a woman. He turned to look at Helen. And he described the note as "the last dastardly act of a murderous woman who had sent his soul hurtling into eternity."

Jimmy's parents, Emmett and Edythe, occupied the front row of the courtroom, his sister, Mabel, and Uncle Gil sitting behind them. Mabel's hand grasped her mother's shoulder in a gesture of comfort.

For the defense, George Warren began with a description of Helen's excellent character. "Is it possible that this clean, white, sweet, good, motherly woman can turn, overnight, into the scarlet woman depicted to you?" Mr. Warren stood in front of the jury box. "I don't believe it. Take the evidence and draw your conclusion. Do not blacken her character on mere conjecture and speculation. I never heard a more bitter appeal to hatred and prejudice in this courthouse." He branded Jimmy as a Jekyll-Hyde personality: handsome, popular and extremely talented but addicted to drinking and drugs. Mr. Warren reminded the jurors of witness testimony that Jimmy had said the Clark home was the only home he had known. Edythe Newton must have seethed from this description. Mr. Warren continued with statements that Mrs. Clark had taken Jimmy into her home and treated him as a son "to fill the void in her heart created by the death of her own son killed at Bougainville, in the wake of the deaths of her husband, father and mother." Mr. Warren stressed that Mrs. Clark was past "the stage of life for romance, desire and lecherous tendencies." Her thirty-six-hour-long grilling by the investigating officers, without counsel, caused her to tell conflicting stories, he offered, because "a lie is a human weapon in time of stress and emergency, used to ward off danger. If she had wanted to lie, then she was a fool to tell the story she did. She could have vindicated herself if she had wanted to."

At 5:35 p.m., the case went to the jury. Dorothy brought in Frances to see their mother and encourage her with a hug. As the supper hour approached, Dorothy, Nancy and Frances left with their mother and uncle C.M. for home to await a call to return to the courtroom. Mr. Warren felt confident the jury would make a quick decision.

The jury filed into the courtroom around 10:00 p.m. "We want to ask a question of your honor. What is the penalty for murder in the second degree?" L.R. Brown, the foreman, asked. Circuit court clerk Charles Booth read the entire charge, which specified the penalty for second-degree murder as no less than five nor more than twenty years in the penitentiary. Word spread, and the courtroom filled. Helen and C.M. took their seats; the three daughters remained at home. At 10:16 p.m., the jury reentered the packed courtroom with the verdict: Helen was guilty of murder in the second degree.

Helen showed no emotion. The only relative by her side was her brother C.M.

Her punishment was recommended at five years in the state penitentiary.

14

THE MURDERESS
AND THE AFTERMATH

Immediately after the verdict was read, the defense counsel moved that "the verdict of the jury be set aside and the defendant granted a new trial on grounds to be assigned in writing at a later date," reported the newspaper. Judge Robertson stated that the court would be in session until May 25. As the date approached, Helen's attorneys withdrew their motion to set aside the jury's verdict.

The morning humidity pressed down on Helen as she entered the courthouse. On Thursday, July 11, the Washington County Circuit Court held her sentencing hearing. Vista Ellen Talbert Clark was sentenced to serve five years in the state penitentiary for the second-degree murder of James Emmett Newton Jr. Judge Walter F. Robertson pronounced sentence at 10:30 a.m. The court held "only a handful" of spectators to hear "the final act of the sensational case." The sentencing had been scheduled for Monday, July 15, but the earlier date may have limited the number of people who knew about or were willing to show up for the session.

The court placed Helen in the custody of a deputy for transfer to the state penitentiary in Richmond. Deputy Sheriff S.S. Atwell left immediately with Helen for Richmond by automobile.

⎯⎯∞⎯⎯

DOROTHY WAS NOT OLD enough to be guardian to Nancy and Frances, so all three girls moved in with their father's brother Ed and his wife, Nannie.

Ed and Nannie Clark lived on a farm with their siblings as neighbors: John Clark, his wife and their children lived on one side, and Lucy Gay Clark lived on the other.

The Ropp and Clark Filling Station continued to operate under R.C. Ropp, C.M. Talbert and Dorothy. A young electrician for Appalachian Power lived with his uncle across from the filling station, and like many other young men, he noticed the blond girl who worked on cars there. Jackson Leonard and Dorothy Clark were married at her uncle Ed's farm on Friday, June 6, 1947, less than a year after her mother went to prison. Immediately, Dorothy and Jackson moved into the house on Valley Street and brought Nancy and Frances to live with them. "As a married woman, Mother could be guardian to her sisters, so they all moved back to Granny's house," Gay Leonard explained. Nine months later, Dorothy and Jackson welcomed their first daughter, E. Gay Leonard.

Gay described the timing of Helen's return to Abingdon. "She was back when I was born in March 1948. She was here at the house on Valley Street." With that milestone, Helen served less than two years. "Aunt Nancy got married on Mother's twentieth birthday, and

Mrs. Leonard

Mr. and Mrs. E. H. Clark of Abingdon, Va., announce the marriage of their niece, Dorothy Ellen Clark, to Mr. Jackson Leonard, Friday evening, June 6, at six o'clock at their country home. Mr. Leonard is the son of Mr. and Mrs. G. N. Leonard of Abingdon.

Dorothy's wedding announcement, June 22, 1947, when her mother was still in prison. *From the* Bristol *(TN)* Herald Courier.

I was born four days later," Gay explained. Nancy married Martin Tate, and the newlyweds moved to Bland County, Virginia, about seventy miles from Abingdon. Helen lived in the house on Valley Street with Frances, who was then eleven. Dorothy, Jackson and their baby, Gay, lived in a rented apartment nearby.

Once Helen returned to Abingdon, the town whispered and talked about the murderess on Valley Street. Frances had the most difficult time of the girls with the rumors about her mother. Since she was still in school, she had to deal with the taunts of other children.

Jackson Leonard worked as a lineman. He was assigned to Damascus and moved his family there. Then he transferred to Scott County, Virginia, and Dorothy, Jack and their children moved to the small town of Dungannon.

Helen Clark in 1967.
Gay Leonard.

"Aunt Nancy went to Bland County and never came back. Aunt Frances married a guy from Scott County and never came back. The only one bold enough to live in Abingdon was Mom," Gay Leonard stated of her mother, who moved back years later. "And I had asked her, 'Mom, how could you live in Abingdon? Go to church in Abingdon? Work in Abingdon? Do all this volunteer work?' And she said, 'I had two parents. It wasn't just Mother. I'm my father's daughter, too.'" Gay talked of how her mother and aunts idolized their father, Hal, and their brother, Hal Jr. They served as inspirations to the girls and set a level of dependability and service that Dorothy, Nancy and Frances strove to live up to.

As Gay grew up in Dungannon, Virginia, she heard nothing about her grandmother's trial or conviction. Her grandmother, mother and aunts never talked of it—not until Gay graduated from Dungannon High School and studied at Radford College. At that point, Gay's youngest sister, Eva, was in elementary school, and Dorothy had moved them back to Abingdon. Their concern was that some of the children at the school would tell Eva her grandmother had been in prison for shooting a man. The family decided to tell Dorothy's daughters.

"I used to try to get them to talk about it [the murder trial]. Aunt Nancy said Granny lost her husband, both of her parents, and Hal (Jr.)." Gay said Nancy believed that stress, worry and nervousness, initiated by the accumulated and concentrated losses, caused Helen to act as she had.

Helen must have received more counseling while at the prison and afterward. She reclaimed her life and family status. Gay remembered her childhood years when she had no idea of Helen's past. Friends and neighbors visited and socialized with Helen. Andrew Summers always made a point to visit Helen when he came to Abingdon from Manhattan.

Helen wasn't a figure for pity or contempt. She was the widow of Hal Clark. That still holds status eighty years later. Although some neighbors and acquaintances still murmured their suspicions of her guilt or innocence, no one outwardly talked about it—as was the southern Appalachian small-town way.

Jimmy, on the other hand, since he was the outsider, was easily blamed for his own death, as he had used alcohol and drugs and become too familiar with Helen. Why would he not move on with his life? Why spend so much time with a woman twice his age or with high school boys? The tragic collective memory concentrates on Helen, not Jimmy. Those who knew and cared for the young marine veteran, popular musician, beloved coach and teacher have passed on. Their children and grandchildren may have never heard of Jimmy Newton and the impact he had on the students in Damascus.

15

THE RUMORS AND SCENARIOS

With her second-degree murder conviction, Helen's unplanned but intentional killing—as the jury decreed—of Jimmy rippled across generations of Clarks and Newtons. The commonwealth attorney's prosecution strategy was built on the motive of jealousy. They did not prove that motive. Yet the jury knew Helen had shot Jimmy and then lied about it. Her motive is still debated, and new theories float among Valley Street residents as they walk by the house.

ANALYSIS AND POSSIBLE SCENARIOS

Jimmy may have been abusing the daughters.

The most common motive—one repeated by locals with confidence, even without any facts about Jimmy, Helen or her daughters—is that Jimmy probably sexually abused one of the daughters.

With the base statistics that Jimmy was twenty-two years old, Dorothy was seventeen and Helen was forty-four, people make the conclusion that Dorothy would have been the most logical woman to attract Jimmy.

"Mother was beautiful," Gay Leornard said of her mother, Dorothy. "People have said that Granny shot him to protect Mother. That he was trying to do something to Mother. So, you know me, I asked if Granny shot that man. Mother said, 'I don't know who shot him. She never admitted shooting him.' I asked, 'Do you think Granny could have shot that man to protect you?' And Mother said, 'That is the most ridiculous thing I have ever heard. Absolutely not. Mother [Helen] was the most selfish person that ever lived. I would have been on my own.'"

Gay explained that she understood why Dorothy had said Helen was selfish. After Helen lost her husband, Hal, and then her mother and her father, all within an eight-month span—add to that Hal Jr. joined the navy and was killed at Bougainville in the Pacific—Helen crawled into her own grief. "She could have stepped up," Gay said, "and raised the kids. Instead, they took care of her. Aunt Nancy took care of the house and cooked, and Dorothy ran the service station." Dorothy wasn't alone with no one to look out for her. "Uncle C. was there for Dorothy, but he drank. He wasn't there to protect Dorothy at the service station. Now, I'll tell you what, she was tough. I would bet nothing happened to her." Friends of Hal Jr. had returned from the war, and they watched out for the girls. "Granny just abdicated. She sank into depression. She didn't have to. She could have dusted herself off and been their mother."

For many years after Gay was told of the murder trial, she tried to get her grandmother, mother and aunts to discuss it with her, but they stayed silent or, at most, vague.

"You know, I've thought about it for years and tried to get all of them to talk," Gay stated. "I'd bet everything I own that he didn't have any kind of sexual relationship with my mother." Gay said Dorothy dismissed any speculation that she could have been the reason for Jimmy's death. "He wouldn't have dared touch her," Gay added. "That was the way she said it. 'He wouldn't have dared.'"

Jimmy saw Helen like a mother,
but she was romantically in love with him.

In the trial, an undercurrent for Jimmy was that he didn't feel close to his mother. From the research on his time before the war, including the work Edythe did with the Viavi Hygiene Company and its principles, Edythe loved her son but pushed him to be an independent man. He never seemed to have a healthy relationship with a woman. His father, Emmett, focused on his work and left the child-rearing to Edythe, which, by all accounts, wasn't her strongest trait. When he walked into the Clark home in December 1944, Jimmy saw three sisters and a mother mourning Hal Jr. The reminders of their son and brother's active and celebrated existence and importance to the family lined the walls of the home: snow skis, tennis rackets, rifles, award ribbons, as well as his desk, chair and books still anchored the entrance hall. Hal Jr. was a presence in the Valley Street house.

Jimmy was born on June 11, 1923. Eighteen days later, on June 29, 1923, Hal Jr. was born. To Jimmy, this closeness in their births predicted his potential place in the Clark family.

Gay Leonard recounted a time when she asked her grandmother why she didn't remarry. "I asked Granny, 'Why didn't you ever date? Why didn't you ever remarry?' It seemed like with four kids to raise by herself, the logical thing would have been to remarry.' She said after being married to Hal, 'Why would I ever look at another man? Who could ever compare to him?'"

Helen was in love with Jimmy, but he had no interest because he was interested in another woman his own age.

Kitty Smyth was the only woman ever mentioned in connection with Jimmy in the trial or by the Newton family. Jimmy's parents stated that he had traveled through Abingdon to see Kitty when he was stranded by a snowstorm in December 1944. Kitty said she and Jimmy had met in December 1943 in the atomic boom town that would soon be Oak Ridge, Tennessee. The *Knoxville News-Sentinel* reported, "A meeting at Oak Ridge started the chain of circumstances that culminated in James E. Newton's killing."

The only other reference to a young woman alluded to a female teacher at Damascus; her father, W.M. Tolley, testified for the defense that Jimmy and another teacher had come to their home to have dinner. Mr. Tolley said he "smelled intoxicants on him" and asked Jimmy and the other teacher to leave. The female teacher, Miss Tolley, may or may not have been romantically interested in Jimmy, but the fact that another teacher was invited appears to show Miss Tolley and Jimmy were only coworkers.

Whether he had a girlfriend his own age or not, Jimmy may not have shown interest in Helen. A widow at the age of forty-four would be a vibrant and healthy woman. She may have craved the affection of a man, no matter the age difference. "Just to get some attention," Gay Leonard added. "She was used to being the pretty, young wife, and here was a man coming into the house, and she wasn't getting the attention."

Helen saw Jimmy as a replacement for Hal Jr.,
but Jimmy disappointed her and broke the fantasy of the perfect son.

If Jimmy had decided he was not a replacement for Hal Jr., or if tensions had risen from him not being able to live up to the legend of Helen's son, he may have told her he was leaving the boardinghouse.

"Whatever kind of relationship they had, whether it was like losing a son or not," Gay Leonard explained, "all the people had left her [Helen] that were ever going to. I know she didn't like it when Aunt Frances got married and went to live with her husband. She wanted everybody to stay right here. She wanted Mother [Dorothy] and Daddy [Jackson Leonard] to come back with me and live with her in her house. None of us were supposed to go anywhere. We were supposed to be with her. There was obviously some kind of big emotional attachment to Jimmy. But who knows what kind?"

Jimmy's attributes that Helen admired included his musical abilities; his service to his country, church and community; his good-naturedness; and his devotion to the people he cared for. But these were offset by his detrimental traits, such as his abuse of alcohol, pain killers and sedatives—things Helen did not abide, especially given her father and brothers' overindulgence of alcohol.

One scenario said that Jimmy had decided to leave Helen's home, either to enjoy more freedoms in Damascus, follow his students to college or move to Manhattan. With Helen's fragile state and feelings of abandonment—even abandonment through the death of her loved ones—she may have tried to force Jimmy to change his mind. The rejection from him could have caused her break.

Helen covered for the real killer.

Family legend includes Helen's original pondering that Jimmy had been killed outside the house, brought up the stairs and placed on the floor.

"She never admitted shooting him. I don't know if she shot him," Gay Leonard stressed. "Uncle C. was her little brother. If you have some kind of racket with Uncle C., or if Uncle C. was protecting Granny or helping Granny after she did it, or if Granny was helping Uncle C. after he did it." Gay stated that the repercussions of Helen being convicted were not as severe as they would have been if C.M. had been convicted of murder. She described her uncle C.M. as "a raging alcoholic after that murder. But apparently, that's genetic. His father [Charley Talbert] drank, but we didn't think Uncle C. did until after that. But then he did. He climbed into a bottle."

The defense team never called C.M. Talbert to the stand. He was the first person from outside the house to arrive the morning Nancy discovered Jimmy's body. Gay admitted the idea that her Uncle C. was involved came from her family tales. "I thought Jimmy had been found in his bed. They always said Granny couldn't have gotten him in bed by herself. Somebody had to help her pick him up and put him in bed. I'm not making this up. I know they [her mother and aunts] told me that he was in bed. I thought he was in bed, covered up."

No other suspect was hinted at during the trial, except for Jack Henderson, whom Roby Thompson asked if he had threatened to kill Jimmy over a relationship with Helen. In that shrewd move, the commonwealth team caused the defense to fiercely object to the accusation of another person who might have shot Jimmy. After that, the jury looked only to Helen and Jimmy.

Helen was in love with Jimmy,
but he had no interest because he was gay.

With the prosecution banking on a motive of jealousy, their witnesses didn't present Jimmy as a libertine, a Cassanova, a handsome marine who would seduce a lonely widow, a trail of broken hearts in his wake. George Warren and his defense team did more to paint Jimmy as an amorous man than the commonwealth. Emory Widener, in closing for the defense, labeled Jimmy as "a big, handsome, talented Kentuckian…a man who took advantage of her [Helen] and her home."

The commonwealth team of Roby Thompson and Fred Parks called witnesses like Emmett Newton, Gil Cowherd and the Damascus boys, who described Jimmy as a young scholar, musician, scout leader, teacher and coach. This portrayed him as a model citizen but didn't tint that image with the passionate hue of a man who could cause a jealous rage in a woman. Jimmy's depiction is almost that of a eunuch within the Clark home and its female residents. This didn't line up with the prosecution's motive of jealousy.

Kitty Smyth stated that Jimmy had asked her to the Kentucky Military Institute's formal dance in Florida during the spring of 1944. Kitty didn't seem the type to turn down a trip or a potential adventure, especially with a campus full of young men and male teachers on a Gulf Coast beach. Yet she did and showed little interest in Jimmy when they were both in Abingdon from December 1944 until his death in November 1945.

Was he gay? The subject would have been taboo in the 1940s. Gay men in World War II, especially those who didn't fit the exaggerated and erroneous stereotypes of a "sissy" or "coward" or the contradictory stereotype of aggressive pursuers of partners that prevailed in the era, could "pass" as straight so officers or fellow soldiers didn't form suspicions. Men in the military didn't have time for gossip. Allan Berube, in his book *Coming Out Under Fire*, explained that fighting soldiers, gay or straight, were "able-bodied men, mostly citizen-soldiers, in their teens and twenties. Who had been trained in combat and sent into battle." These men served alongside each other, protecting each other—southerner, northerner, farmhand, taxi driver, college student, musician, mechanic, Christian, Jewish, atheist, gay or straight. They had a job: win the war. And the military relied on each man to achieve this goal.

Relationships were established, especially in the buddy system of combat. Berube explained that the "open affection expressed toward each other" was captured in wartime photographs. The "combat soldiers' acceptance of one another's pairings and physical intimacy was more a recognition of their need for closeness in life-threatening situations than any conscious tolerance of homosexuality" by the military command. But he added that a gay veteran stated, "People ended up lovers. The ship was crawling with them. It was an accepted thing."

Jimmy had a close relationship with his marine buddy Clarke Beetlestone. Intimate and devoted, the two spent days and nights together. Jimmy's promise to Clarke to visit the Beetlestone family in the New York area was one of the reasons he made the trip that left him stranded in Abingdon in the snowstorm. Then when Clarke was declared MIA and then presumed dead, Jimmy abandoned his plans of returning to Florida. His shipboard pact with Beet to move to Manhattan had been scuttled. He seemed to resign himself to the wants and needs of Helen.

But enough was enough as the eunuch on Valley Street. In Damascus, Jimmy carved out a life for himself. He enjoyed the company of the other teachers and his football team. He partied with the boys and spent nights on a cot in the locker room. On the evening of his death, did he tell Helen he wasn't interested in her romantically? Did he tell her he was moving out? This would not have provoked her into shooting him. Or did it?

Had he realized he would never be able to play the part of a husband? A teacher and coach could not be exposed as homosexual in 1945. Did someone threaten to out him? Could that have triggered an emotion so deep and terrifying that he attempted suicide? Helen may have walked in when he had the gun and they struggled, as she said. But this would not explain her behavior and lying.

Did her own PTSD from the losses in her life cause her break down from witnessing Jimmy's death? She continued to create new lies for the next few days. Had she blocked the moment she pulled the trigger and created situations that took the blame from herself?

⎯⎯⎯⎯⎯⎯

AN EDUCATED AND RESEARCHED
YET SPECULATIVE CONCLUSION

Two lonely and damaged people found themselves with a loaded gun between them. Helen could not have physically overpowered Jimmy. She did not fire the gun from the bedroom doorway; the shots were close. She must have surprised him. He probably had his back to her. The forensics on the distance of the gunshots tell that the bullet hole in the middle of Jimmy's back was caused by a gun "held against the coat with some pressure." The other shot to his back came from fifteen to eighteen inches away. The two shots to his chest, one that entered his body from the right edge of his jacket and the other through his left shoulder, both came from a gun that was thirteen to fifteen inches away. The front wounds could have been self-inflected, but the shots would have been awkward for Jimmy. It is not possible for the back wounds to have been self-inflected.

Helen had to have had the gun in her hand for the two shots in his back. Even with the testimony of Deputy Browning that said the "squeezer" safety feature of the .32-caliber Smith and Wesson pistol kept it from going off by itself, it may have fired accidentally if it was held by its grip handle. The squeezer feature was used to keep the small hand of a child from shooting the gun, not an adult.

Helen may have walked up to Jimmy while he faced the bed or wardrobe. She could have pressed the gun against his back and fired. As he pitched forward away from her, she could have shot again. He may have turned toward her in shock. This would have placed her at the right distance for the two front wounds. He then would have fallen to the floor on his back.

The gun had to have been grasped in a shooting position, a hand wrapped around its grip; its safety lever then had to have been squeezed while a finger was on the trigger. The gun could not have been discharged while gripped any other way—like if it was being grabbed in a struggle to take it away from another person.

The gun could not fire four times in a struggle. Helen shot Jimmy.

The motive couldn't have been simple. Dorothy swore that Jimmy had never sexually abused her. This would fall in with his homosexuality. The only person Jimmy truly cared about was Clarke Beetlestone. When Beet died in the war, Jimmy's plans for their future died, too. Helen's feelings for Jimmy may have been maternal or romantic, possibly both at different times of their relationship. Jimmy imagined that Helen, an older woman, would be a safer romantic partner than a woman his own age. Kitty expected more from Jimmy than he was willing to give her. He saw Helen as a friend, companion and confidant.

He may have felt close enough to Helen to entrust his sorrows, fears and desires—or lack of desires—with her. What would have been her reaction to his rejection of her passion, whether he disclosed his sexual orientation or not? Her state of emotional and mental stability collapsed after the loss of so many important men in her life: her brothers Robert and Frank; her husband and the love of her life, Hal; her father, Charley Talbert; and, finally, her beloved son, Hal Jr. In the year they were together, Jimmy served as a substitute for all those men in her life.

Jimmy shattered her pieced-together future. He said he would move from the house, maybe going to New York City, where he could be part of Andrew Summers's world. In New York, he'd be close to the Beetlestones and could be part of Beet's family. Or he may have decided to return to Florida or to enroll in college with the seniors graduating from Damascus. He wasn't just leaving the boardinghouse; he was leaving her. Helen's abandonment issues surfaced. She could not let Jimmy desert her.

Her defense team may have understood this. Embree Potts and Tom Hutton had known her and Hal for most of their lives. George Warren and Emory Widner, along with the prosecution attorneys, Roby Thompson and Fred Parks, socialized and worked in the same circles that Hal Clark had. The complexities of the widowed Clark's mind were too multifaceted for the jury to understand, so they saved Dr. Wright's testimony for last.

Mental health physician Dr. George Wright's testimony held an unspoken weight with the twelve men of the jury when he stated Helen's menopause contributed to her actions during and after the murder. The jury consisted of eleven farmers and one merchant between the ages of twenty-nine and sixty-seven, and all were married. Menopause as a contributing factor, to these men, had to have been confusing, since most women didn't talk about this change of life with their husbands. Yet they knew what it was, and they wanted no part in discussing it. They understood Helen needed help, but they also realized she wasn't innocent.

The verdict of second-degree murder allowed Helen to be back home with her daughters in less than two years. Although the families' stigma never faded, the Clarks and Newtons endured. If this situation played out today, with what we know about PTSD, both military and civilian, Helen may have sought mental health assistance to deal with her losses. And maybe Jimmy would have done the same and then lived a long and happy life.

BIBLIOGRAPHY

Ancestry.com. "U.S. Federal Census Collection." https://www.ancestry.com/search/categories/usfedcen/.

———. "U.S., Marine Corps Muster Rolls, 1798–1958." National Archives at Washington, D.C. https://www.ancestry.com/search/collections/1089/.

Baum, G.R., J.T. Baum, D. Hayward and B.J. MacKay. "Gunshot Wounds: Ballistics, Pathology, and Treatment Recommendations, with a Focus on Retained Bullets." Orthopedic Research and Reviews 14 (September 5, 2022): 293–317.

Berube, Allan. *Coming Out Under Fire: The History of Gay Men and Women in World War Two*. New York: Free Press, 1990.

Bristol Herald Courier. "Clark Prosecution Rests; Dismissal Denied." May 10, 1946, 1.

———. "Clark Verdict May Be Rendered Today." May 13, 1946, 1.

———. "Damascus High to Install Football." September 16, 1945, 7.

———. "Frank H. Talbert Dies at Abingdon." December 31, 1928, 3.

———. "Most of Virginia Roads Cleared of Snow Drifts." December 15, 1944, 1.

———. "Mystery Surrounds Slaying of Young Damascus Teacher." November 20, 1945, 1.

———. "School Principal of Rye Cove Tells Story of Disaster." May 3, 1929, 1.

———. "Snow Blanket Covers Bristol Area." December 11, 1944, 1.

Bristol News Bulletin. "Bizarre Story Is Related by Mrs. Clark in Newton Death." November 21, 1945, 1.

———. "Ellen Clark Is Sentenced to 5 Years in Prison." July 12, 1946, 1.

———. "Newton-Clark Death Motive Still Unproven." May 9, 1946, 1.

———. "Quiz Clark Venire About Death Penalty Scruples." May 7, 1946, 1.

Brown, Douglas Summers. *Recollections of Old Abingdon*. Abingdon, VA: Historical Society of Washington County, 2009.

Courier-Journal. "Middletown Boy Wins Kentucky Drivers Contest." August 10, 1940, 9.

Cozens, Eloise. "McCray Takes Over as 'Youngest' Mayor." *Miami Herald*, April 9, 1956, 35.

Crosby, Mary Jane. "Memories of Abingdon's Nursing Students." *Historical Society of Washington County, Virginia Newsletter* 42, no. 2 (May 2020): 4–5.

Daytona Beach Morning Journal. "Weekendiana." March 13, 1945, 3.

Daytona Beach News-Journal. "Chatterbox." January 21, 1945, 8.

———. "Chatterbox." July 1, 1945, 6.

Decuers, Larry. "WWII Post Traumatic Stress." National WWII Museum. June 27, 2020. https://www.nationalww2museum.org/war/articles/wwii-post-traumatic-stress.

Fogg, Rodney D., U.S. Army, major general (retired). Interview by Greg Lilly. June 15, 2023.

Ford Motor Company. "National Finals, Ford Good Drivers League, 1940." National Archives. August 1940. https://catalog.archives.gov/id/93419.

Hagy, James William. *History of Washington County, Virginia to 1865.* Abingdon, VA: Historical Society of Washington County, 2013.

Hicks, Evelyn. "Trial Coverage (Multiple Days)." *Bristol Herald Courier*, May 6–13, 1946.

Journal Virginian. "Abingdon Visited by Heavy Snow." December 14, 1944, 1.

———. "Dorothy Clark County Queen." June 22, 1944, 1.

Knoxville News-Sentinel. "Chain of Circumstances Began in Oak Ridge." May 14, 1946, 14.

———. "Virginia Woman Tells Weird Shooting Story." November 22, 1945, 10.

———. "Woman Gets 5 Years in Killing of Coach." May 14, 1946, 1.

Lancaster Medical Heritage Museum. "Pharmacy: Chemicals, Medicines, and Cures from N to Z." 2023. https://lancastermedicalheritagemuseum.org/.

Law, Hartland, and Herbert E. Law. *Viavi Hygiene.* San Francisco, CA: Viavi Company Inc., 1908.

Lebanon News. "Abingdon Woman Is Indicted in Slaying of High School Coach." November 30, 1945, 1.

Leonard, Gay. Interview by Greg Lilly. July 20, 2022.

Paridon, Seth. "Life on Guadalcanal." National WWII Museum. October 2, 2017. https://www.nationalww2museum.org/war/articles/life-guadalcanal.

Richmond Times Dispatch. "Jury to Get Murder Case on Monday." May 12, 1946, 22.

Symonds, Craig L., PhD. "Episode 8: Guadalcanal: Jungle Warfare." *World War II: The Pacific Theater.* Chantilly, VA: Great Courses, August 13, 2020.

Tackett, Brittany. "Drug Use in Wartime." American Addiction Centers. November 30, 2022. https://recovery.org/addiction/wartime/.

Washington County Journal. "Robert Talbert Meets Horrible Death While Shifting Cars." May 1, 1914, 3.

ABOUT THE AUTHOR

Greg Lilly grew up in Bristol, Virginia, and then lived in Charlotte, North Carolina. The rich storytelling tradition of the South captivated him, and he began writing. He first turned to creating short stories after plot lines emerged from the technical manuals he wrote for a large family-owned corporation. He has published short stories and novels. Today, he lives and writes in Abingdon, Virginia.

www.GregLilly.com